TROUT TRACKS

We would like to also take this opportunity to acknowledge the traditional territories upon which we live and work. In Calgary, Alberta, we acknowledge the Niitsítapi (Blackfoot) and the people of the Treaty 7 region in Southern Alberta, which includes the Siksika, the Piikuni, the Kainai, the Tsuut'ina, and the Stoney Nakoda First Nations, including Chiniki, Bearpaw, and Wesley First Nations. The City of Calgary is also home to Métis Nation of Alberta, Region III. In Victoria, British Columbia, we acknowledge the traditional territories of the Lkwungen (Esquimalt and Songhees), Malahat, Pacheedaht, Scia'new, T'Sou-ke, and W̱SÁNEĆ (Pauquachin, Tsartlip, Tsawout, Tseycum) peoples.

TROUT TRACKS

• ESSAYS ON FLY FISHING •

Jim McLennan

Illustrations by Lynda McLennan

RMB

First Edition

For information on purchasing bulk quantities of this book, or to obtain media excerpts or invite the author to speak at an event, please visit rmbooks.com and select the "Contact" tab.

RMB | Rocky Mountain Books Ltd.
rmbooks.com
@rmbooks
facebook.com/rmbooks

Cataloguing data available from Library and Archives Canada
ISBN 9781771603652 (paperback)
ISBN 9781771603669 (electronic)

Cover design by Lara Minja, Lime Design
Interior layout by Colin Parks
Printed and bound in China

We acknowledge the financial support of the Government of Canada through the Canada Book Fund and the Canada Council for the Arts, and of the province of British Columbia through the British Columbia Arts Council and the Book Publishing Tax Credit.

Canadä Canada Council for the Arts | Conseil des arts du Canada | British Columbia | British Columbia Arts Council An agency of the Province of British Columbia

To my two grandsons,
Levi and Xander, who at 5 and 7
already know that the
heart of knowledge is curiosity.

CONTENTS

FOREWORD

When I was 13, I didn't play team sports. I was more interested in the river that flowed under the freeway just a couple of miles from my house. I could ride my bike there quite easily, and spent many days just throwing rocks, floating sticks and, of course, fishing. In those days I had a spinning rod, a bobber, some lead weights and a jar full of bright red salmon eggs. In order to afford all that swag, I procured a part-time job at a pet store taking care of aquariums full of tropical saltwater and freshwater fish. When I wasn't feeding goldfish to piranhas, scooping fish for customers or provoking the Siamese fighting fish (*Betta splendens*), I was down at the river trying to catch trout.

Unfortunately, I was terrible at it. The Bow River was nothing like an aquarium; it was a vast galaxy of unknowns, at times roiled with sediment and dangerously deep and fast, at other times dark and mysterious. Little of what I saw ever translated into usable information, and as a result I plunked away uselessly for many summers, and only occasionally caught Rocky Mountain whitefish.

That started to change when I got my driver's licence and was allowed to ramble about in my mother's green 1976 Ford Granada. One of my first stops that summer was at a small store I found listed in the Yellow Pages under the fishing category. Inside those magical doors were rods and reels, the likes of which I'd never seen before; bins of impossibly small and fuzzy lures; shelves of fat fishing lines; and what looked like wetsuits of all sizes and colours hanging by their suspenders. "Are they swimming with the fish, or trying to catch them?" I wondered.

I quietly bought a magazine with an article about the Bow River and left the shop. But I went back to Country Pleasures many times just to listen to the banter between the shop owners and their customers.

There seemed to be three proprietors. Two of them made me a little nervous. I feared that if I asked the wrong questions, they'd find out I was an imposter, and throw me out of the clubhouse forever. But one of the shopkeepers seemed to enjoy it when people asked stupid questions – not so he could ridicule them, but as sort of an icebreaker to get a conversation started. He'd say things like "I thought the same thing but found out..." or "It sure seems like that, but..." I was comfortable talking to him because he admitted to asking stupid questions himself at one point or another, and was happy to share what he'd already learned.

I was a broke teenager, and not a good customer, but then again, I don't think Jim McLennan was ever much of a salesman. He was born to be a teacher, and that's what he's done in his long career of guiding, writing, filming and instructing. I was just one of thousands he's helped along the way.

When I was still a teen, he directed me to the books, magazines and VHS tapes that helped me make giant leaps forward. For me, he was the curator of all fly-fishing knowledge – a librarian of sorts. He loaned me VHS tapes such as *Fly Fishing Alberta Canada's Bow River with Lefty Kreh* and *The Essence of Flycasting* with Mel Krieger. He also gave me book recommendations and sold me Norman Maclean's *A River Runs Through It and Other Stories*.

By the time I reached university, I was, like most other kids my age, just trying to figure out what to do with my life. I skipped a lot of classes to go fishing. I read and reread everything Jim McLennan wrote in *Fly Fisherman* and *The Alberta Fishing Guide*. And then in 1987 Jim published the award-winning book, *Blue Ribbon Bow*, and I was powerfully struck by the true relationship between trout streams and fly fishers – they need us to survive, but in many cases we need them even more. Not just to catch fish but to find ourselves.

Jim has always been able to artfully provide instruction, entertainment and humour, but most important, he's been able to inspire us. In all of his writing, from *Blue Ribbon Bow* to the *Trout Tracks* book you hold in your hands now, he's able to masterfully inch us toward a higher purpose and give us a clearer understanding of our role as fly fishers.

In this book of essays, Jim writes about getting a thank you from a homeless man who claimed, "Fly fishing saved me."

I think that sentiment resonates with most of us. Fly fishing certainly saved me, or created the person I am today. To a large degree, my life outdoors was predicated and modelled on the things I read in books and magazines – and most of those aspirations came from the keyboard of Jim McLennan in the most formative period of my life.

When I finished *Trout Tracks* I was again inspired, and also overjoyed to think that there's a new generation of fly fishers coming into our sport right now, just as I did so many decades ago. And I'm grateful we have Jim McLennan to lead them.

ROSS PURNELL
EDITOR/PUBLISHER, *FLY FISHERMAN* MAGAZINE
OCTOBER 2021

ACKNOWLEDGEMENTS

Thanks to Rocky Mountain Books, especially Don Gorman for allowing himself to be talked into publishing this project, and Peter Enman, who edited it with a sure hand and made what you read better than what I wrote. And thanks to the magazines and publications that ran these pieces initially: *Fly Fisherman*, for which I've written since 1985; *Fly Fusion*, for which I've written features and the "Water Marks" column since 2004; *Maclean's*, Canada's newsmagazine; *The Alberta Fishing Guide*, which has been a required resource for Alberta anglers since 1971; and Anchored Outdoors, April Vokey's wonderful network/platform/website. Thanks also to long-time friend and fly fishing success story Ross Purnell for writing a moving and humbling foreword.

Lynda's art has made this an especially attractive book visually. Thanks, Lyn, for the magic you provide in these pages, and everywhere else.

PREFACE

This is a book I wrote without realizing I was writing a book. It's a collection of some of my magazine pieces written and published between 2010 and 2021. They've been gathered into sections based loosely (very loosely) on topic or subject matter. There is no overriding theme or message here, except perhaps that fly fishing has a way of grabbing people, making them think, making them enjoy, making them appreciate and helping them learn. I hope that will suffice.

1. Places

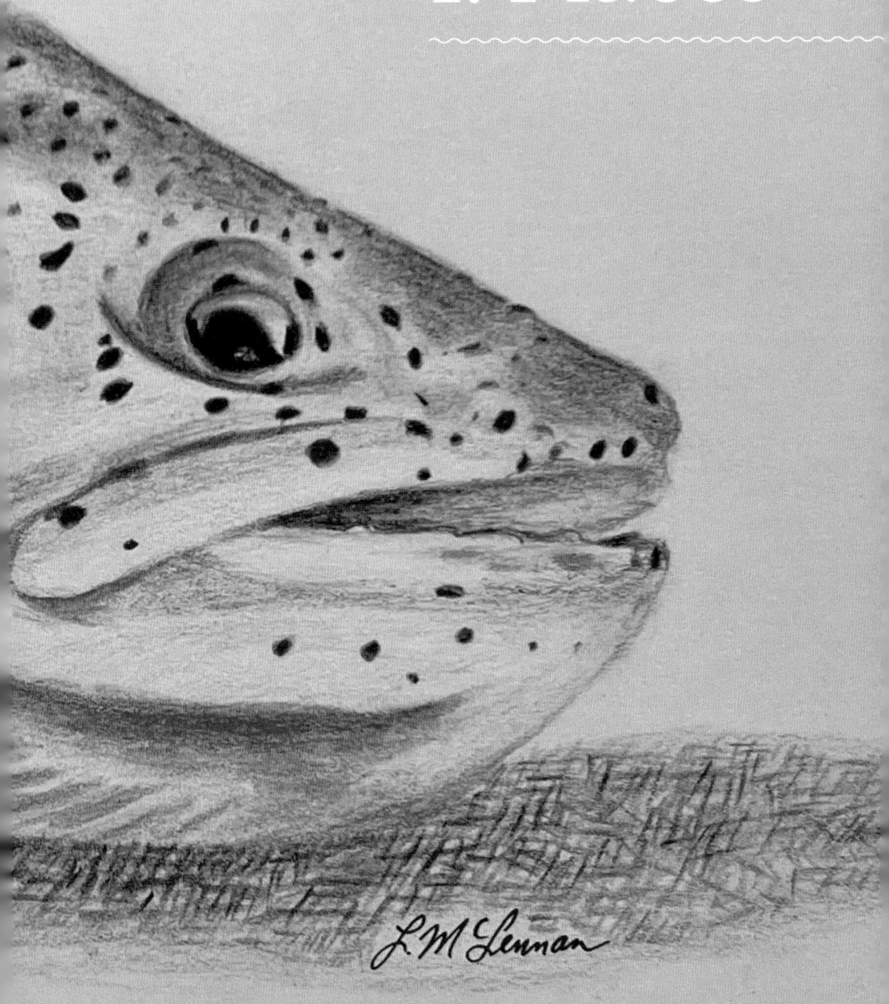

INSTITUTES OF ADVANCED LEARNING (2016)

Through the years I've been lucky and have fished with some true experts who, while they didn't say "sit on the bank and listen while I explain how to do this," certainly helped me by answering my ceaseless questions and demonstrating while they were fishing. Today you can get formal help from an instructor, you can watch videos, read books and magazines or watch a friend who knows what he's doing.

But along with people there are also places that are especially suitable for learning. These are usually lakes or streams with good numbers of fish and circumstances that provide a lot of opportunity to fish in a particular way.

My first and most direct encounter with this came one April when a friend took me to the spring creeks of Montana's Paradise Valley, near the town of Livingston. These are high-profile streams, where paid access is available to a limited number of anglers each day. The streams – Armstrong and Nelson's Spring creeks – are small but have high populations of fish and reliable hatches of mainly small insects that bring the fish to the surface. The streams get fished a lot and the trout are very selective.

Before going there I was familiar (I thought) with how to fish to rising trout, but that first day on Armstrong's some of the finer points were revealed. Even though my friend had fished these creeks many times, we hired a guide (and there's a lesson there too).

When we got to the stream the first morning, midges were hatching and fish were sipping daintily in a shallow flat in front of the fishermen's hut. Everybody who fishes this stream has a go at these fish and as a result they're nearly impossible to fool. The guide, Al Gadoury, positioned me up and across from the risers and rigged me up with a 12-foot, 7x leader and a size 20 midge emerger that looked like a tiny piece of dryer lint. Then he showed me how to use a downstream delivery with a reach cast (which I was familiar with but hadn't used much) to get a perfectly drag-free, fly-first drift over the trout. We changed flies from time to time (slight variations on dryer lint), but when I did things Al's way with his flies I caught a few fish, and that signifies success on these creeks.

After lunch the spring hatch of *Baetis* mayflies started and the fish rose even more. Al took me away from the flat and left me at the tail of a long, bouncy pool while he went to help my friend. When the hatch peaked, dozens of trout were gulping the little grey duns that danced down the current. The red sides of feeding rainbows sliced the surface everywhere. It looked like a case of shooting fish in a barrel, but was instead an exercise in total frustration. I made cast after cast to feeding fish, sure I was getting plenty of perfect drifts. Yet the only acknowledgement from the trout was an occasional polite pause in feeding while they waited for my fly to drift over and get out of the way. I was hunched over, fishless, oblivious to everything but the rising trout, when I heard Al's voice from behind me. "How're you making out?" I didn't answer, as I was pretty sure he had been watching and knew perfectly well how I was making out. He had me change flies a few times, finally getting to a René Harrop No Hackle. But after a couple of casts to one fish he wanted me to switch to a different fish. Al knew that after these trout have seen the same fly a couple of times their selectivity dials get cranked up, but if you leave them alone for a few minutes they forget all about you. So the best chance at a fish is on the first couple of casts. Again, when I did it Al's way I caught some good trout. I learned things that day because I was both in the right place and with the right person.

On that trip and subsequent ones to the same streams I've learned most of what I know about fishing small flies to difficult fish. The lessons are transferrable and have served me well in many places since.

Other places have other lessons. Big rivers can teach us about fishing streamers or about fishing from a drift boat. Small, brushy brooks can show us how to fish in tight quarters. In a small, rocky river not far from my home I finally broke through the frustrating Catch- 22 of nymph fishing, which says that to be successful you have to be confident, yet to be confident you have to be successful.

These places and others have the one thing that's crucial to learning a new technique: abundant opportunity to use it. If you only get to try something a few times in a day, the learning curve is pretty flat. But with frequent repetition comes increasing success, and with success comes confidence, and confidence is foundational to learning. On spring creeks and rich tailwaters there are often rising fish everywhere, so if you foul up on one, it's only a matter of seconds before you can try another.

If you believe, as I do, that learning is one of the primary reasons for fly fishing, waters like these are classrooms of the first order.

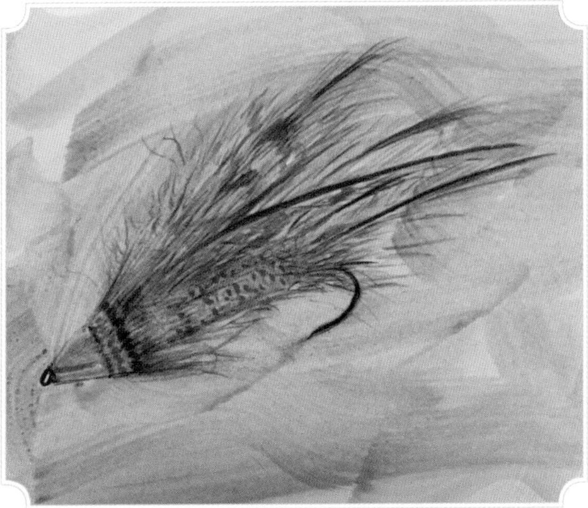

FLY SHOPS (2015)

Fly shops are one of the main cogs in our sport, and it's hard to imagine fly fishing without them. There's the small Mom and Pop (or maybe just Mom or just Pop) operation that's in a tiny town with some good fishing nearby. The store dispenses sound river-knowledge and has great local flies, but is a little light on high-ticket items like premium rods and fancy reels. Most of the shop's customers arrive pretty well "tackled up" and mostly need to augment or restock their flies, leaders, floatant and any gadgets they lose, or maybe get some new waders if their old ones give up during the trip.

These kinds of shops usually offer a guide service but may also provide shuttles for people floating the river without guides, and might make you a lunch to take on the water, seeing's how they're making them for their guides anyway. Some have a few rooms for rent in the back of the store. Sometimes they're seasonal operations, open only during fishing season, or morphing into ski shops in winter.

Another type of shop is the one near a major "fly-fishing destination." It's a sizable store either in a small town very close to the fishing or in a larger city not far away. The high traffic drawn by the famous fishery allows it to carry extensive inventory with plenty of high-ticket items, including gifts, clothing and art.

There are also "urban" fly shops, which are in major cities that may or may not be near great fishing. These are larger, year-round operations, and the fancier ones are sometimes called "boutique fly shops." Those near good fishing have two types of customers. They have visitors who come to the area to fish, but they also have a large base of local customers who live in the city. These are the people who come by on their lunch breaks and keep the shop going in the off-season. The shop has strong Christmas sales, offers winter in-store events and fly-tying courses, hosts trips to exotic destinations, and perhaps brings in fly-fishing celebrities to give presentations in the off-season. While these shops do more dollar-volume business than the smaller ones, you can be sure that their space is both larger and more expensive, and they need to do more business to pay for it.

Fly shops are safe houses for fly fishers when they can't be on the water. Think about it. You're supposed to be going to the mall to pick up some mundane household stuff, but for no apparent reason you find yourself in the fly-fishing store that's adjacent to – or at least not more than a few miles out of the way of – the store you're supposed to be going to.

There's a reason they draw us in like they do. Fly shops exude fly fishing, and if you can't be doing it, the next best thing is probably talking about it with other people who have the same interest. Those people might be other customers or the staff in the shop. So fly shops play a valuable role beyond simply providing equipment to the sport's participants.

I'm reluctant to spill the beans here, but because I have some familiarity with fly shops from the inside I can tell you that there's also a "dark side" that the general fly-fishing public knows nothing about. Here it is: Fly shops are businesses. They have to pay rent; they have to order product. They have to pay for that product (and pay for it on time, if they want to continue carrying that brand). They have to put up with pesky and pushy sales reps. They have to make the shop look good. They have to keep the shop clean. They sometimes have staff problems. Yet, when you walk into Joe's Fly and Tackle, you'll see no evidence of any of this, for it's imperative that the shop project a constant vibe of fish, flies and fun. Owner Joe will appear to have not a care in the world and will be ready to answer every fishy question you can muster and will pretend to believe every ridiculous and exaggerated fish story you deliver. A fly shop, perhaps more than most other businesses, is expected to dispense and promote optimism and pleasure at all times, because one of its responsibilities is to provide you with a break from the stresses of *your* job.

But after the customers have left and the store is empty, the manager returns to the office and resumes the squabble with the landlord who wants to raise his rent 25 per cent, or with the supplier who has just informed him that the 250 dozen flies he was assured he'd have in June will be delivered in October if there aren't any more production problems.

Running a fly shop is never easy. And it might be more difficult today than ever, thanks to a number of things, including and especially, the Internet. Online shopping is taking its toll on brick-and-mortar fly-fishing stores throughout North America. So consider some of the things fly shops provide you with beyond just equipment, and do what you can to support them. I think we'd all prefer that the shop be there the next time we stop by.

FISHING LODGES (2017)

Among the many "institutions" in our sport – those things that are inherently connected to it, like fly shops, fly-fishing guides, fly-fishing towns, fly-fishing literature and art – one of my favourites is the fly-fishing lodge. They have a long tradition in our sport, going back at least to Atlantic salmon lodges of the eastern US and Canada in the 1880s.

Lodges that provide comfortable accommodation, meals and guided fishing are now fixtures at many of the best and most popular fly-fishing destinations throughout North America. They are also common at freshwater and saltwater destinations around the world. Some you can drive to, some you must fly to, others can only be reached by boat. Generally speaking, the more remote the location, the greater your anticipation and the more enduring the experience.

Lodges are in the business of creating lifelong memories. The top lodges simply know how to do things right. Because the fishing they provide for their guests is still... well, fishing, it's never completely reliable, so these lodges follow the axiom of controlling the things they can control, and doing their very best with the things they can't. So the food, the accommodation, the ambience and the service are as good as they can be, and the guides do all they can to provide guests with the best fishing available in that place at that time.

Strangely, it's sometimes the unexpected little things lodges do that make the strongest impressions. In a previous life, filming my first fly-fishing TV series, the crew and I stayed at a rustic lodge in northern Saskatchewan. Although the fishing and everything associated with it was as good as we had hoped, the first thing that comes to my mind when I think of that place is – coffee. Early each morning before any of us were awake, one of the staff placed a thermos of fresh, hot coffee on the porch outside each guest's cabin. It was a perfect way to begin a day of fishing in a grand and mysterious place. Each morning after the first I found myself thinking (or maybe dreaming) about that steaming thermos as I started to slide toward consciousness.

I visited the same lodge in New Zealand twice, several years apart. On the second visit I mentioned to our hostess how much I had enjoyed the food she had prepared on my first trip. With that she said, "Oh, that's nice to hear. Would you like to know what we fed you last time?" Then she pulled out her notebook and read me all the meals she'd served us the first time around, so I could request repeats of my favourites. This was done for every guest that visited the place.

One of the best non-fishing parts of the lodge experience are the stories that are told over "happy hour" drinks or during meals. As you might expect, the stories get more bizarre and hyperbolical as the evening goes on, and only some of them are about fishing. If you can refrain from participating for a moment to look around the room (which is probably decorated with fly-fishing and outdoor memorabilia, photographs, art and taxidermy), you'll see smiling faces and hear loud, honest laughter.

Many fond and lasting friendships have their beginnings at a fishing lodge. It might be with another guest, one of the guides with whom you make a strong connection or the people who run the place. Repeat get-togethers either at the same place or a different one are often planned on the spot.

This is all on my mind because as I write, Lynda and I have just returned from one of our favourite lodges, Northern Lights, on Quesnel Lake in northern BC. It's a place I've visited several times, initially using it as a base for the filming of *Fly Fusion TV*. I might have been feeling a little guilty about the fact that I had been there several times and Lynda had not been there at all, so this fall we made a trip together and Lynda was finally able to experience what I have come to love at this place. I came off as kind of a hero (not an automatic occurrence) because everything was pretty much as I said it would be. We had great fishing, ate great food, met new friends and left with great memories.

I might be making it sound like I frequently trot around the world, staying at the most luxurious and expensive places at the best fly-fishing destinations. It's not exactly like that. My financial circumstances usually push me toward do-it-yourself trips, but through my work (yes, work) I do sometimes find myself in places I couldn't visit otherwise.

I guess the lodge trip is the flip side of the do-it-yourself trip. There are good reasons for a DIY trip (possibly financial), and for many of us, visits to fishing lodges are once- or twice-in-a-lifetime events. But we can make them happen if we take the same approach we do to other significant vacations, which is to plan early, save for as long as it takes to collect the money, and then – go.

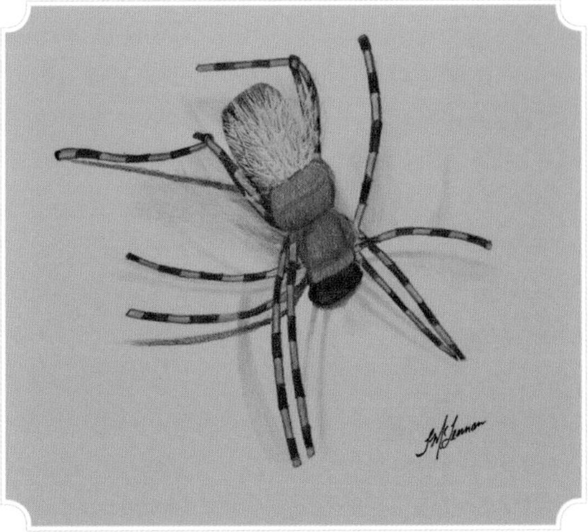

MONTANA (2016)

For a time I travelled much of the Rocky Mountain West in both Canada and the US on business, and as much as I could, kept an eye on the trout streams I found myself crossing with great frequency. I decided to create a "top ten list" of the most attractive streams in the West. My criteria were simple, and had nothing to do with my experience fishing the streams. This was simply a list of the rivers that called my name the loudest and made me most *want* to stop and fish them. The ones that topped the list were the Big Hole River near the town of Melrose, the Blackfoot near the town of Lincoln, and the Madison between Quake Lake and Ennis. I didn't plan it this way, but it turns out they're all in Montana.

I know that these streams are great fisheries as well as beautiful to look at, but in truth fishing equal to that in Montana exists through much of the Rocky Mountain West, in Wyoming, Idaho, Colorado, British Columbia and Alberta. But when we think of western fly fishing it seems we've been programmed to think of Montana first. Montana's reputation permeates fly-fishing culture to the point that it's an automatic entry on everyone's list of "must fish" destinations. So is Montana's tourism department doing an especially good job, or is it really a great place to fish? The answers are yes, and yes. But it's sometimes a mistake to go to Montana expecting better fishing than you have at home. Instead you should expect fishing that's different from what you have at home.

One of the things that makes it different in Montana is that fly fishing is an important thread in the fabric of the state's identity. I once escorted a New York City business associate on his first trip through western Montana. When we drove past the tiny village of Craig on the Missouri River, he looked over from the Interstate at the semi-decrepit but humming hamlet and said, "What do these people do out here?" The answer is that many of them are involved in the business of fly fishing. If you hang around awhile it seems that everybody is either in the business themselves, is related to or is friends with someone who's a guide, works in a fly shop, drives a shuttle vehicle or works at a fly-fishing lodge.

The state has clearly recognized the economic benefit to being a fly-fishing destination and happily flaunts its association with the sport. There are at least two glossy, upscale Montana outdoor magazines that seem to be funded by large colourful ads for expensive (very expensive) real estate on famous trout streams. I suppose this supports the opinion that Montana has been "discovered." The more curmudgeonly among us would go so far as to say it has become "yuppified." After all, there are cappuccino shops in every small Montana cowboy town these days – some of them right in fly shops. All this bothers some people, especially those who came to love the place before this happened.

For this and other reasons I usually visit Montana during what's called the "shoulder seasons," which means early enough in spring that the crowds haven't arrived yet or late enough in the fall that the crowds have pretty much cleared out. Some of these trips provide good fishing and some don't. I've been blown off the Missouri in September and snowed in on the Bighorn in April. But these trips have provided a view of Big Sky Country that's unvarnished, a little more raw, a little more gritty than what the tourism brochures depict. And maybe this is what I like about those seasons. They give me a little glimpse at what Montana was like before it became trendy. At these times of year the other fly fishers I encounter are likely to be similarly hard-core lifers who are there at that time for the same reasons I am.

Like every place with a big reputation as a fly-fishing destination, Montana has two categories of water: the places everybody knows about, and the places everybody doesn't know about. The streams and lakes in the first group are great and should be sampled, but reputations of such weight come at the expense of solitude. You'll have some company when you fish them. The waters in the other group require more investigation, which always carries the possibility you'll wind up pursuing a wild goose, but solitude is likely yours if you take a suggestion from a cattle rancher who "used to fish a bit" or follow a hunch you get by staring long enough at a topographical map.

If you've been at it awhile, you know that fly fishing comes with off-season cravings too. The idea of an April trip to the famous spring creeks near Livingston, Montana, begins when I'm reminded of the smell of the woodstove that heats the fly shop I prowl through on the mornings when it's a little too early and a little too cold to fish yet. A fall trip to the Missouri comes unexpectedly to mind when I realize the days are getting shorter and I can smell both new snow from the high country and grain-harvest dust from the prairie. I'm not always able to indulge these cravings, but one thing's sure: if a fishing season comes and goes without even a brief trip to Montana, that season goes into the books as incomplete.

LAKES (2018)

I sometimes feel guilty because I don't write much about fly fishing in lakes. I always hoped that people would assume I knew plenty about lake fishing but avoided writing about it because I didn't want to show off. But alas, the real reason I don't write about it much is because I don't do it much, and consequently I'm somewhat less than an expert. I make this confession reluctantly, fully aware that it ruins my shot at being perceived as a complete fly-fishing master.

It's not that I don't like lake fishing – I cut my fly-fishing teeth in mountain lakes of Canada's national parks. But my fishing then was a most unsophisticated variety and my principal strategy for trying to catch a fish in a lake has remained the same from the early days till now. I tie on an Olive Woolly Bugger or something similar, throw it out there somewhere and strip it back in. If I'm feeling especially avant-garde I might tie on a dry fly, throw it out there somewhere and not strip it back in.

So, no, I don't have a depth finder or fish locater. I don't tie my thermometer to a string to check the water temperature at different depths. I don't carry four different densities of sinking fly lines. My boat doesn't have two anchors (oh wait, I don't have a boat).

But this unrefined approach did lead to my one and only moment of glory as a lake angler. About 20 years ago I was fishing near Kamloops with fly fishing's lake-guru, Brian Chan. Brian was doing his thing – sampling the water, taking its temperature, studying his fly box, fussing with his leader. I did my thing too – chucking an olive Woolly Bugger randomly into the lake. I caught four fish before Brian caught any (at least I remember it as being four; there's a slight chance it was one). So of course this went down in my memory as "the day I out-fished Brian Chan." In truth I out-fished him for about 20 minutes. For the rest of that day he caught all the fish, and while doing so he graciously and patiently explained in a pleasant voice the numerous reasons why my Woolly Bugger had worked for a short time and had stopped working for a long time.

Some people think still water is easier to fish than moving water, but they're wrong. When I look at a lake, I mostly see a blank slate. There are some obvious things to notice, like bays, islands and other bits of "structure," but most of what you need to know is hidden beneath the surface. To be consistently effective, a lake angler should be familiar with and know how to take advantage of things like thermal stratification, eutrophic something-or-other, littoral zones (different, I'm told, from figurative zones), chironomid emergences (including how to spell and pronounce chironomid), how and when damselflies emerge, what colour the leeches are in different parts of the lake at different times of year.

The hot thing in lake fishing these days is chironomid fishing. That's fishing with imitations of the lake-midges that are important and populous in most trout lakes. As I understand it, the ascending pupae is the stage preferred by the fish and most imitated by the angler. The pupae make their way from the bottom of the lake to the surface at a specific time of day and at a specific speed. Once the water's depth is determined (using the aforementioned depth finder or a pair of forceps tied to a line and lowered to the bottom), a leader of the same length is attached to the fly line. Then, when the colour and size of the pupae are determined (by what means, I'm not sure), an imitation is chosen, a cast is made and the fly is allowed to sink to the correct depth, which is confirmed when the leader hangs straight down from the end of the floating fly line. This can take some time. You might want to bring a newspaper. After the fly has reached maximum depth, it's retrieved very slowly so it rises toward the surface. It's slow-motion fishing, and this is the part that causes detractors to say it's "like watching leaves change." And while I confess to making similar comments because it's fun to do so, I know that's mostly sour grapes. The method's serious practitioners – Brian, Phil Rowley, Joe Cunningham and others – have experienced enough success to make them trust in the patience that's required to fish this way.

The other thing my "lakey" friends know is what to do when something that's working stops working. They don't seem to have to go back to the drawing board. They'll look at the sky, peer into the water knowingly and say something like, "I think they've switched to damsel nymphs." Then they tinker with their tackle for a bit before getting right back to catching fish.

As I said, I don't fish lakes much, and it occurs to me that some people might think that's because I'm a snob, but I wouldn't want you to get the wrong impression. That's not it at all. I'm a snob for completely different reasons.

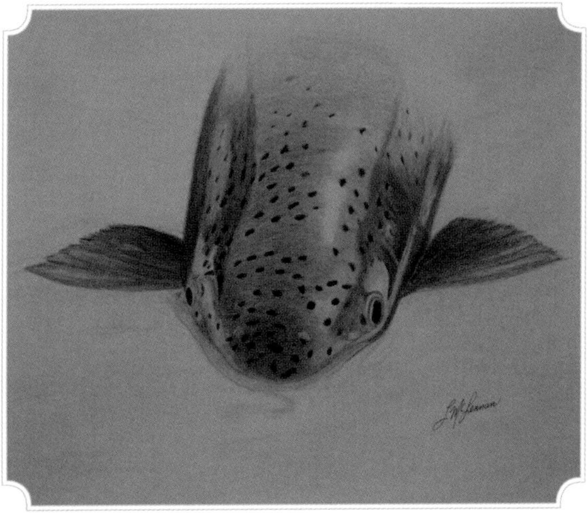

A FAMOUS RIVER (2016)

Lynda and I have just returned from fishing the Missouri River, near the town of Craig in northwestern Montana. Now if you weren't a fly fisher, but somehow found yourself in Craig about the middle of June (though that probably wouldn't happen unless you were lost or confused), you'd wonder what you'd stumbled into. The place hums with activity. There are more vehicles pulling drift boats than not, and most everyone wears "the costume" of shorts, sandals, sweat-stained ball caps and raccoon-eye tans. In the only bar or the only restaurant you'd notice that nearly all conversations focus on trout, flies, fish, leaders and who caught (or lost) what earlier that day. You'd also notice some odd vanity licence plates – BAETIS, DRFTBT, BRNTRT. In this town of 30 permanent residents (2013 census) there are three fly-fishing stores, all busy.

What you've stumbled into is prime time on one of North America's "famous" trout streams. It's the Missouri that flows through Craig, but other streams produce similar microcultures throughout trout country. Farther east in Montana it's the Bighorn, over in Idaho the Henry's Fork, in Wyoming the Snake, in Colorado the Frying Pan.

So what qualifies these trout streams as famous? A number of elements contribute, starting with high populations of good-sized trout. They also receive frequent gushing descriptions of the fishing in magazines, websites and social media, and are frequently featured in TV shows and films. The publicity attracts lots of fly fishers, and spawns fly shops and guide services that further promote the fishing. The nearest community becomes a "trout town" where the culture of fly fishing is evident at all times. They're the streams everybody's allowed to mention by name.

Another quality of many famous fisheries is strong and reliable hatches of insects the fish like to eat. Lynda and I scheduled our Missouri trip to coincide with the hatch of pale morning dun mayflies so we could feed our addiction to casting over rising fish.

But there were a lot of other people looking for the same thing, so we had to manoeuvre a bit to find a spot on the river where there were few other fishermen. The first day we walked in to a nice flat near town. Drift boats went by regularly, but nobody disturbed the area we were fishing. When we got there about 9:30 there were a few flies on the water and a few fish rising, and we caught some using small Pheasant Tail Nymphs just beneath the surface. As the hatch gained strength and more fish rose, we caught a few on PMD emerger patterns. Then we started to see "cripples" on the water. For some reason this hatch produces a high percentage of duns that don't survive; they lie on the surface like spent spinners, except they aren't spinners, they're dead or "crippled" duns. We caught a couple of rainbows with PMD cripple patterns and then these flies stopped working. It was now 2:00 p.m. and the PMDs were about done. The fish kept feeding, though, and a close look showed that the tiniest of western mayflies, the ones called (or formerly called) *Pseudocloeon,* had taken over from the PMDs. Tiny (size 28?) and nearly transparent, these are insects I've learned to hate. I simply can't catch fish that are eating them. Because we had stopped catching fish and the weather was hot, we went back to town to have something to eat and cool off. But the morning went down as a definite success.

I went out again that evening with intentions of "hitting" the caddis hatch. When I got to the water there were some caddis buzzing around the streamside vegetation, but on the water the PMD duns were back in much greater numbers than we'd seen earlier that day. Say what? This hatch is supposed to be a late morning or midday event. I'll spare you the embarrassing details, but after two hours of constantly casting to rising fish, I had zero takes. On the walk back to the truck I met another fisherman who was just "looking things over." He carried no rod, but when he heard my sad story he told me that the Missouri has a hatch of flies that look very similar to pale morning duns but emerge in a completely different manner. Okay, I'll take that; maybe it's why I couldn't catch them. It was good to have an excuse provided by a stranger.

On our final day we floated the river with a friend, starting very early. There was virtually no PMD emergence, and the best activity was when some rusty spinners hit the water in big numbers and the fish came up nicely – for about 30 minutes. Unfortunately, when this happened most of the good dry-fly spots had already been claimed by other anglers. We found a place with some rising fish just in time for the spinner-fall and feeding activity to peter out.

Our final evening started with Lynda catching a beautiful, big, steadily-rising rainbow on a spent caddis pattern. We then went fishless until I noticed with surprise PMD cripples on the water again. I changed flies and caught two nice fish in the last 15 minutes of our trip.

In my world, casting to actively rising fish is the purest form of fly fishing. And on rivers like the Missouri, while you sometimes don't catch a lot of these fish, you nearly always get a lot of chances at such fish, and I guess that's the real attraction.

So over three days we caught a surprisingly small number of fish, considering our expenditure of time, effort and money. We had blazing hot weather, unexpected and incomprehensible hatch activity, and educated, maddening fish that at times made it clear that they simply would not be fooled.

So we'll never do that again.

Yeah, right.

2. Bugs, Real and Fake

THE SECRET FLY (2017)

The fly that's tied to the end of the leader is the focal point of the sport. It's where hackle meets H2O, the final link in the chain between the fish and us. And that's probably why it seems so natural to worry and fret about flies the way we do. Our obsession with the details of fly pattern is rooted, I expect, in the eternal hope that we will someday find – or better yet create – a pattern that is truly magical and works where and when others don't. It's a search for the holy grail of fur and feather.

It's hard to tell which group is more particular, fly tiers or fly buyers. I had ample opportunity to observe both while working behind the counter of a fly shop, and I'll say here that I think it's the tiers. This is going to sound worse than I want it to, but fly tiers used to drive me crazy. It would often start when the latest new pattern showed up in a fly-fishing magazine, with tying instructions and a materials list that included several items nobody had ever heard of. I was sure that most of these oddball ingredients could be easily and successfully replaced with things more common, but when Mr. Obsessive-Compulsive

Fly Tier arrived in the shop, carrying a copy of the magazine, I couldn't convince him of that. If he used common mallard flank feathers instead of identical-looking Siberian Double-Crested Cormorant flank feathers, for instance, the fly wouldn't really be an authentic Smith and Jones Cormorant Caddis, now would it?

This problem also arose frequently in regard to hook styles. In the photograph in the magazine, the fly appeared to be tied on a standard dry fly hook, but the guy who invented the pattern and wrote about it used a Sanagucci 2546AAA hook – a hook that an hour or so of research revealed is a standard hook, but with a barb that's 26 per cent shorter than standard. So when Mr. OCFT asks if I have any Sanagucci 2546AAAS, I respectfully point out that in our area the law requires us to pinch the barbs, making barb-length moot, so perhaps he'd like to try our standard dry fly hook, which is of the highest quality. He wants no part of it, and if we don't have the correct hook, would we please order some for him.

Then there is colour. If something is supposed to be pale avocado green, medium dun sage just won't do. I'll never forget the day Mr. OCFT asked me to show him our red marabou. When I handed him a package the colour of Santa's suit, he looked it over for a moment and said in a quiet voice that dripped with disappointment, "Jim, that's not red."

We also love to speculate about what flies look like from the fish's perspective, taking into account things like refraction, distortion, the way colour is affected by the position of the sun or the depth of the water, the presence or absence of air bubbles clinging to the body of the bug, and the materials used to imitate the air bubbles that may or may not be attached to the body of the bug.

Of course if we follow this scrutiny of fly patterns to its logical destination, we run up against the real fly in the ointment, if you'll pardon the expression. If we believe our imitation must have the correct number of tails and the exact shade and density of mottling on the ventral side of the bug's third abdominal segment in order to fool a trout, what are the trout supposed to make of the leader sticking out the front end of the fly? Even worse, what do they think the big, curved metal thing hanging out the back end is?

This question has been troubling fly fishers for years, and until recently I've not heard a plausible answer. But I met someone who has a good theory. Dave Ames lives in Montana, where he's retired from guiding fly fishers to write. He is the author of a number of fine fly-fishing books, including *True Love and the Wooly Bugger,* and *A Good Life Wasted*. Dave has researched trout's brains, senses and behaviour, and frequently delivers his findings to fly-fishing clubs in a program called "The Mind of the Trout: How Fish Perceive, Think and Remember." Dave has learned that trout's eyes function in a manner similar to a camera, with a very short depth of field at close range. This means that when a trout gets close enough to eat a fly, only a very small part of the fly is in clear focus. So Dave believes that trout don't care about the leader or the hook because they don't see them. I like it.

I'll wrap it up here, except to remind you to watch for my next article, in which I'll reveal the tying recipe for my soon-to-be-famous Triple Mega Micro Emerger. Anybody know of a source of natural chartreuse mole fur?

WHOSE FLY BOX? (2015)

I've always enjoyed looking inside other anglers' fly boxes. Even though it seems a little improper, as if I'm snooping through somebody's bedroom, when I do it I often see new fly patterns that I didn't know about, or am reminded of flies I like that I'd forgotten about.

When I teach a fly-fishing class the students often want to look through my fly boxes, perhaps thinking they'll get some sort of secret insight or at least will get those same things I look for when I do my snooping. But this is generally a big letdown. With slight embarrassment, I open my boxes and then watch the students try to conceal their disappointment. My flies are very ordinary and very disorganized, and the boxes look a lot like the junk drawer in my kitchen. No secret inspiration there.

I never snoop through other people's fly boxes without their permission, of course, but that brings me to my real point. There are some fly fishers' boxes that I don't simply want to look at, but instead want to possess. For that to happen I suppose I'd have to steal one. And this troubling idea isn't just for the purpose of possibly connecting with something of historical significance from an important tier. I would probably save some of the flies and frame them, yes, but I'd learn some things by finding out what's in the boxes, and I'd have some great flies to fish with too.

The late Gary LaFontaine's fly box would probably be full of many of his original patterns like the Mess and the Mohawk, flies I've seen in his books but never used because they're too unconventional to be available in fly shops. I'd find out what sizes and colours he carried, and would probably see by the numbers of each which ones were his favourites. But what I'd really be curious about would be the flies he carried that he never wrote or talked about. What about those? Did he not talk about them because they were untested or because they didn't work, or... did he not talk about them because they *did* work and he didn't want the rest of us to know about them?

Brian Chan and Phil Rowley would probably be at the top of most lake fishers' hit lists. I think they use the giant boat-boxes favoured by many lake anglers, so it might be harder to execute the heist, but if you got your hands on one of these you might have a thousand flies – chironomids, damsel nymphs, leeches, water boatmen – row on row on row.

But the fly box I'd go to the greatest lengths to "acquire" would belong to René Harrop. A renowned Idaho tier and fly fisher, he has developed his fly-fishing methods and fly patterns largely to take on the sophisticated trout of the Henry's Fork of the Snake River near Last Chance (yes, that's the name of the place), Idaho. This is some of the most technical water anywhere, and its trout are among the most selective. The river is broad and flat, with a nice gravel bottom. You can wade across it in many places and it has diverse and prolific hatches that sustain the fish and drive fly fishers crazy. It's one of the places where the "pattern versus presentation" discussion doesn't cut it; here both must be perfect. You need a deadly accurate cast to get the fly right to the fish and then you need a perfect dead-drift of the fly. The latter is difficult to achieve because by early summer the weeds on the bottom of the stream wave gently just beneath the surface and create a maze of small but maddeningly difficult currents that prevent that perfect dead-drift. And along with these physical challenges are the entomological challenges. The rich water produces simultaneous hatches of different but sometimes similar insects. Because the trout see anglers every day of the season they're very careful about what they eat, and the fly fisher must figure out exactly which stage of which insect the fish are feeding on and choose an acceptable imitation. This water is known throughout the fly-fishing world for its difficulty, and someone once said it's the only stream where you can hear fly fishers cussing in several different languages.

Waters like the Henry's Fork have taught us much of what we know about trout's surface-feeding behaviour, and are where specialized techniques like the downstream dry-fly method were developed.

Harrop has been at the centre of all this for decades, and his fly patterns, many of which are highlighted in his book, *Learning from the Water*, show a delicate elegance I've not seen from many other tiers. It's not that his patterns are detailed duplicates of the real bugs, but that they carry the fragile, translucent qualities of the real insects, and are beautiful to the eye as well as convincing to the fish. He uses mostly natural materials and considers how the materials appear and behave in and on the water. He has developed and tested patterns for each stage of each important insect on the Henry's Fork, coming up with flies like his CDC Floating Nymph and CDC Captive Dun.

Would you steal a fly box if you were sure you wouldn't be caught? Or even if you weren't so sure?

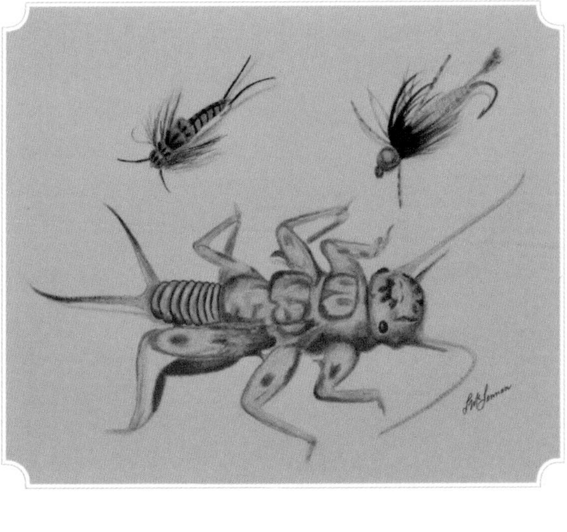

TRICOS (2015)

The late summer hatch and spinner-fall of tiny *Tricorythodes* mayflies is one of fly fishing's most dramatic events. Under ideal conditions on ideal mornings immense swarms of spinners shimmer in the air over the water and riverbanks in clouds that look like grey smoke, millions of busy wings producing an audible hum. Spinners find their way into your shirt, into your ears, behind your glasses, into your sandwich. The fish like them and move into the stream's shallow edges and long flats, hovering just beneath the surface and tipping up and down as fast as physics and hydrology allow. Small bits of food mean lots of rises, and fly fishers like that.

Tricorythodes are found in many trout streams throughout North America, in eastern streams like the Delaware and Ausable, in Pennsylvania's limestone streams, and in waters like the Missouri, Bow, Silver Creek and the Henry's Fork in the West. Like all trout-bugs, tricos require specific habitat. They need slow currents, a stream bottom with some silt, and a good batch of aquatic plants. The best waters are rich spring creeks and tailwaters, though they are also found in freestone streams where conditions and habitat are suitable. They don't seem to exist in numbers in high-altitude, rocky-bottomed and nutrient-poor streams. Trico nymphs feed on phytoplankton and diatoms, along with tiny bits of organic debris that they scavenge by rooting through the silt on the stream bottom.

The emergence begins about midsummer and lasts to mid-autumn. It appears to be one long hatch, but that's because tricos are multi-brooded. One "class" emerges through the first half of that period and another in the second half. When the big show starts, the male duns emerge first – often through the night – to be joined in early morning by the females. Tricos spend a very short time as duns, moulting into spinners early in the morning. Spinners swarm over and along the water, increasing in numbers until the air temperature warms to the right point to send them to the surface of the water. The critical air temperature for this is thought to be about 20°C, though I've seen spinners on the water on autumn days when the air didn't get that warm. Because of the sheer numbers of flies on the water, it's the spinner-fall that's most important to fly fishers.

There are some other facts about tricos that are interesting at least, and also of some value to fly fishers. Some examples: They're often thought of as having white wings and black bodies, but it's the males that have the black bodies, while the females have olive abdomens and dark thoraxes. The huge swarms above the water are males. Mating takes place in the air. After mating, the females move to streamside vegetation to allow the eggs to “ripen,” before returning to the water to oviposit a few minutes to a half-hour later.

The populations of tricos seem to cycle on some streams. In peak years dense spinner-falls occur each morning for six weeks or so, but the magnitude of the event sometimes declines over a few years, before recovering gradually. This may be standard operating procedure for tricos, or may be caused by factors like drought or changes in water chemistry that occur naturally or through Man’s various activities.

One of the persistent mysteries about tricos is why some streams have them and other seemingly similar streams nearby don’t. For example, some spring creeks near Bozeman, Montana, have good trico numbers, yet the more famous spring creeks just a few miles away – Armstrong and Nelson’s – don’t. There doesn’t seem to be a clear reason for this, though one theory from Edmonton entomologist Rob Hinchliffe is that slight variances in water chemistry and nutrient cycling affect the tricos’ available food sources. Another theory, from Montana fly fisher Rick Ruoff, is that tricos require a certain amount of seasonal variation in water temperature and if the stream doesn’t have it, tricos aren’t there.

Though the spinner-fall is the main attraction for most trico addicts, it’s unwise to completely overlook fishing to the hatch of duns. Hatching often starts late in the evening, well after the sun is off the water, and continues through the night. You can fish late into the evening or hit the water very early in the morning when duns are still emerging and the spinners have yet to come to the water. I've also had good fishing to hatching duns on cool days when the spinner-fall doesn't amount to much because the air doesn't get warm enough.

The best trico fishing comes in the heaviest spinner-falls and those occur on the best trico days, which have bright, warm, calm mornings. Cooler weather delays or severely reduces the intensity of the spinner-fall, and wind can blow the spinners away from the river.

As summer progresses spinner-falls occur later and later in the morning. When the hatch begins in mid-July or early August, spinners might be on the water by 8:00 a.m. Around Labour Day they might come down around 10:00, and by late September it could be noon before spinners come to the water. All these times are subject to weather, and particularly air-temperature variations.

When the flies are thick on the surface the fish like to hold in shallow water along the streambanks, or just beneath the surface in slightly deeper water midstream. They find a lane of slow, steady current that delivers lots of flies and rise subtly but frequently, making the most of an easy meal.

If the fish are feeding on duns, you should try low-floating imitations like a Trico Comparadun or a Trico Thorax. I'm not attracted to the idea of fishing a trico nymph, but that doesn't mean it can't be done, and tiny Pheasant Tail Nymphs will likely work.

When a full-on trico spinner-fall is occurring, the number of flies on the water can be overwhelming. This raises the question of whether it makes sense to use an accurate imitation of a spinner or to use a pattern that stands out from the crowd of naturals. When there's a constant stream of real flies coming over the fish, does it make sense to put one more in there with them? Even if your imitation is perfect, simple mathematics says the odds are slim that the fish will take your fly rather than another natural. With other hatches of small flies – blue-winged olives, pale morning duns – I carry and use a number of intentional imitations. But because of the sheer density of flies in a good trico spinner-fall I usually choose a fly that stands out from the naturals and gets the fish's attention because of it. I use an imitation of another small insect the fish have been seeing and eating recently. In many places this means a caddis. If you're fishing a trico spinner-fall in the morning, you probably could have been (and perhaps were, if you don't need much sleep) fishing a caddis emergence the previous evening. I often use a #18 dark caddis on trico mornings because it's usually visible on the water. Some people (my wife, for instance) use small ant patterns, often in red. The small caddis or ant gets the fish's attention because it's different from all the other bugs.

If you want to remain "pure" and use an imitation of a trico spinner, there are plenty of patterns to choose from. They'll all have long tails and spent wings. The wings can be made of poly yarn, Z-Lon, other synthetics, or white hen saddle hackles. You'll want to carry some with black bodies to represent the males, and some with olive bodies to represent the females, and to have them in sizes 18 through 22. A good trick is to use a Double

Trico – two trico spinners tied on a single #14 hook to represent a pair of bugs. This appeals to the fish's greed and also lets you use a stronger hook. Double Tricos are not available in all fly shops, but they're easy to tie.

Generally your spinner pattern should float flush in the surface film, but it's okay if it sinks just beneath the surface. The real ones eventually sink too, and the fish eat those as well as the ones right on the surface.

The best outfit for trico fishing is the one in the under 6-weight range that you can cast most accurately. In big, open streams I use a 5-weight, and in smaller creeks, either a 3- or 4-weight. I'm most accurate with an 8½-foot rod rather than a 9-footer. Perhaps the most important consideration is the leader. It should be on the long side, but you must be able to deliver the fly consistently and accurately in the conditions of the day. It's easier to turn over a 12-foot leader when the air is dead calm than when there's a persistent breeze. The tippet should be 5X or 6X, occasionally 7X, and fluorocarbon if you prefer. It should be about three feet long to allow a good natural drift of the fly.

When tricos are "on" you can find single fish, small groups or larger pods of trout working the spinners. While it's most exciting to see a pod of a dozen or more big fish wallowing like pigs at a trough, you may be better off with a single or a pair of trout. It's a little like decoying geese to a blind – too big a flock means too many eyes looking down at you and a greater chance that one bird will see something it doesn't like and spook, taking the whole group with it. It works much the same way with pods of rising fish.

Your best approaches for trico eaters are to cast upstream, or across and down, depending on the situation. In small creeks, you'll probably have no choice but to fish upstream, but in larger streams you may be able to take a position up and across from the fish. By wading quietly into casting position and staying far enough from them to be out of their sight, you can use a reach cast to drop the fly upstream of the fish. At the conclusion of the cast your rod will be pointing nearly straight upstream. As the fly drifts to the fish, you achieve a drag-free drift of the fly by moving your rod tip downstream as the fly drifts on the current. If the fly goes over the fish without being eaten, let it swing off to the side, carefully pick up, false cast so the spray doesn't shower the fish, and make another delivery. This method doesn't require the pinpoint accurate casting that upstream fishing does. In fact you can intentionally cast beyond the line of current the fish is holding in, then drag the fly back with your rod tip until the fly is in the proper lane. Then start following the fly downstream with the rod tip. Be sure to do this well above the fish so they aren't spooked by your actions.

This is a very effective way to convince fish to take your fly, because the fly drifts over the fish before the tippet does. This helps fool fish that are leader-shy. There are, though, a couple of drawbacks to the method. Because you're facing the fish, when you raise the rod to set the hook, you pull the fly *away* from the fish's mouth, and this lowers your hook-up rate.

It's imperative that you wait until the fish has taken your fly and turned back down before you raise the rod tip to set the hook. Do this gently.

The other drawback arises when you're fishing to a pod of rising fish. If you're standing upstream of them, you have little choice but to drift the fly toward the fish that's farthest upstream in the pod. If that fish is hooked, it will turn and run down through the rest of the group, and that will be the end of the pod. I suppose this is only a drawback if you're greedy.

If you're casting upstream to the fish, you must overcome the handicap of showing the fish the tippet before showing them the fly. Some experienced fish, which you're quite likely to have in these situations, just won't eat a fly that obviously has a string attached. I believe the fish can see the tippet no matter how fine it is. The trick is to make the fish focus on the fly and not notice or care about the tippet. I only know one way to do this and it was shown to me by the great Montana fly fisher George Anderson. When a fish is holding near the surface and rising frequently, George stands directly downstream of the riser and makes a cast so the fly lands about a foot above the fish. The fish has very little time to "evaluate" the imitation and sometimes eats it seemingly before it's had a chance to reject the idea. It sounds a little odd, but it does work if you can make deadly accurate casts consistently. Another advantage to this is that you can get a lot of drifts over a fish quickly, because the drifts are so short. And, if you're fishing to a pod of fish (and are greedy), you can start with the one on the outside and farthest downstream.

If you hook that one, it will often peel out and downstream without disturbing the rest of the pod.

In any trico fishing, it's difficult to see your fly, especially if you're using a realistic imitation of the spinner. Your fly simply gets lost among the horde unless you see it land on the water. Visibility is better if you use something other than a trico pattern. If you are using a trico spinner, fish it as a dropper off a slightly larger, visible dry fly, or attach a tiny piece of bright indicator yarn on the tippet about a foot from the fly.

Trico fishing is considered one of the most challenging types of fly fishing for trout. And it often is, but a fly fisher can learn plenty from the experienced trout that know the ways of the tiny white-winged blacks.

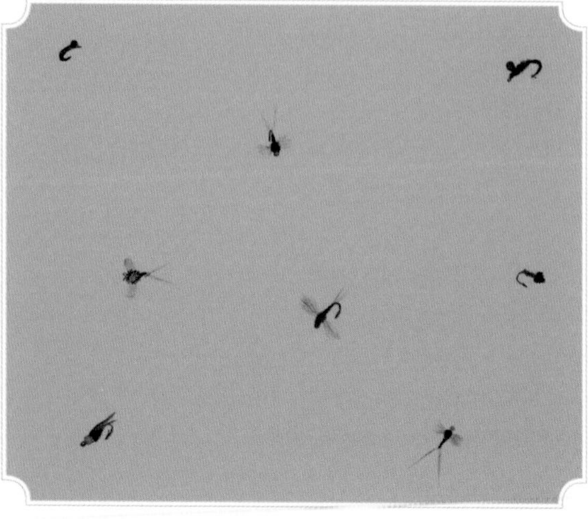

THE TRUSTWORTHY PMD (2017)

When I was learning to be a fly-fishing guide in the mid-1970s, my water was the Bow River in Alberta. Like many young guides, I felt that becoming a fly-fishing guide meant that I'd really arrived and had made something of my life. The feeling was temporary. Anyway, being, I hope, a responsible sort, I knew that I had a lot to learn, about both my river and my new craft. This, of course, meant that I could easily justify the many hours and days I spent fishing – er, researching – on the Bow.

Initially, like many Bow River fly fishers of that time, I considered the river primarily a streamer river. But fairly early on in my, uh, research, I began to see trout – lots of trout – feeding on the surface on the river's long flats and glides. It was late June when I first saw this, and I noted easily that the bugs causing all the fuss were pale, yellow-olive mayflies, about size 16. I imitated them with the closest thing in my fly box, which was an eastern pattern, the Light Cahill. This fly fooled the then-unsophisticated rainbows of the Bow, but I knew that the pattern had been devised to imitate an insect we didn't have. I wanted to know what these flies really were, and luckily the landmark fly-fishing entomology book, *Selective Trout,* by Michigan anglers Doug Swisher and Carl Richards, had been published in 1971. The book has a significant chapter on the insects they dubbed "pale morning duns," and though I couldn't with entomological certainty confirm that these were the mayflies I was seeing, all indications, including the fly's appearance, distribution, habitat and hatching season checked, and that was good enough for me. Pale morning duns they were. In more recent times, more information has been gathered about PMDs, notably by Oregon fly-fishing writers Rick Hafele and Dave Hughes in their great reference book, *Western Mayfly Hatches.*

As the years went by I found these mayflies on other streams and had good fishing in numerous places, and since then I've learned from experience and other fly fishers that it's a hatch of great importance throughout western North America.

Though it's not unanimous, most fly-fishing entomologists, including my bug guru, Rick Hafele, consider pale morning duns to be comprised primarily of two species of mayflies: *Ephemerella inermis* and *Ephemerella infrequens*.

In freestone streams emergences begin around the recession of runoff, which varies with latitude and altitude. In spring creeks and tailwaters, the pale morning dun is an early to mid-summer hatch that lasts a long time – often as long as six weeks.

They are found in some numbers in nearly all western trout streams. The reason is that they thrive in water with rocky or gravelly bottoms as well as in streams with heavy vegetation. So they're happy in freestone streams, tailwaters and spring creeks. The heaviest hatches come from the latter two, as they usually have the water richest in nutrients.

PMD nymphs are chunky crawlers and an olive/brown colour. They have three tails, and are imitated well by variations of the Pheasant Tail Nymph in size 14 or 16.

These insects emerge in the "conventional" mayfly fashion, the nymphs making their way to the surface where the nymphal skin splits and the dun works its way out of its former body and former life. They spend considerable time at the surface in the emerger stage, struggling to make the transition into duns. At this time they are extremely vulnerable to trout, as they're trapped at the surface and can't fly until completely emerged. I believe this is why emergers are so important. After seeing a few fully emerged duns fly away just before they get to them, the trout learn that bugs in the emerger stage don't do that. Emergers never get away. My favourite PMD emerger pattern is Tom Rosenbauer's CDC Rabbit's Foot Emerger, and I fish it without floatant, watching the spot where it lands for the gentle take of a trout.

The duns are about size 16, sometimes smaller later in the hatch, and a pale, watery olive colour, though that varies somewhat from stream to stream. PMDs in Colorado's Frying Pan River, for instance, have a reddish tinge, perhaps because of the red colour of the rocks in the stream. There are many good imitations of the duns, but two of my favourites are a

CDC Comparadun and a Thorax Dun. Emergences occur at just about any time of day, but they are most often a middle-of-the-day event. Hatches are heaviest in smooth water, which is often especially plentiful in spring creeks and tailwaters. In freestone streams you'll find the most bugs hatching in the less turbulent sections.

One quirk of a typical PMD hatch is the number of "crippled duns" that it produces. These are fully emerged, winged duns that die on the water, perhaps from "tipping over" and becoming trapped against the surface film. It's common to see half or more of the duns in this state, lying sideways on the surface with one wing up, or in the standard spinner position (even though they are duns) with wings spread out horizontally on the surface.

The spinners usually come in two colours according to gender. Females retain the colour of the dun, but males are usually a rusty brown. Egg-laying flights and spinner-falls can occur in early morning or late evening. A #16 Hen-Wing Spinner or Poly-Wing Spinner works well, but carry them in both pale olive and rust colours, for the fish might take one but not the other. The pale olive spinner doubles as a perfect crippled dun imitation.

PMD hatches can be fished with most of the conventional fly-fishing methods in use today. The nymphs are usually drifted beneath indicators, sometimes with weight on the leader to get the flies near the bottom. In cases where fish are clearly visible in the water you can ditch the indicator and watch for the fish to open its mouth when you know your nymph is in the right spot.

Emergers, dun and spinner patterns are reserved for times when the fish are feeding on the surface. It's sometimes tough to determine which of the surface-stages the trout are feeding on. Be sure to first check the surface of the water carefully. The duns are so obvious that they can mask the presence of emergers or spinners. You might find more than one stage of the fly drifting in the surface at the same time, in which case you must watch the rises. If they are fairly bold and you see the trout's head break through the surface, it's probably eating fully emerged duns. If the trout just bumps the surface, never actually breaking the film, it's probably taking emergers. Rises to spent spinners are almost in-between. The trout will expose the very tip of its upper jaw, but nothing else, making a beautifully delicate, elegant rise.

A completely drag-free drift of your imitation is essential, and you'll have to choose your casting position carefully and utilize whatever casts and mends the situation calls for. It's an advantage to be able to achieve this drag-free drift from a number of positions: across, across and down, across and up, and directly downstream of the fish.

Trout can get very picky when PMDs are about, especially on popular streams. For that reason it's a good idea to carry a number of different imitations of each stage of the natural. And don't get too cocky when you finally figure out what one trout wants. That doesn't mean his buddy five feet away will eat the same thing. You're often forced to start over with each individual fish.

One of my favourite memories of PMD fishing is of a morning I spent alone on the Missouri River in Montana. Lynda was teaching a class of beginning fly fishers back at the house we rented, and I was on my own for the day. For once my timing was good, and the bugs started coming off nicely shortly after I started working my way up a small side channel. I caught several PMD-eaters that day, but most memorable were a 20-inch rainbow and a 20-inch brown that were taken consecutively just a few feet away from each other, on different PMD imitations. After releasing the brown I went back to town to bask in the glory.

Pale morning duns are a universally important western mayfly – a favourite of trout and fly fishers alike. Why? Because they live in nearly every western stream you're likely to fish; because the trout respond to them, even if the hatch is sparse; because the hatch occurs in the daytime when you're likely to be on the water; because the hatch goes on for a long time; and because every stage of the insect is eaten by the trout and is therefore "imitatable" by the fly fisher.

What more could you ask of a bug?

EIGHT MONTHS OF BIG DRIES (2018)

I realized the other day that there are enough big insects on western streams to make it feasible to fish an entire summer without using a fly smaller than size 10. You'd have to switch rivers a few times to avoid lulls between hatches on any one stream, but what would be wrong with that? You could fish a whole season and never need your reading glasses to change flies.

Why are big flies so good for both trout and fly fishers? From the trout's perspective, a big bug is an economy-sized chunk of protein. The fish gets more calories for less effort, so it's worthwhile taking one bug if there's only one to take. From the anglers' perspective, aside from the obvious visibility advantage, we like the fact that trout develop a recollection or at least a lasting recognition of large insects, which means that they'll take our imitations even if they aren't actively feeding on those insects at that particular moment. Fish take big dries when the hatches are in progress and for a week or two after they've ended. So you can catch a fish on a grasshopper pattern on a day when there aren't many natural hoppers on the water, as long as the fish have been seeing some in recent weeks. That equation doesn't work for smaller insects. You won't get very far fishing a tiny blue-winged olive when there aren't any corresponding naturals around.

The first stop on the western Big-Fly Trout Tour might be in west central Montana near the trout-town of Missoula, which is within spitting distance of at least four major trout streams. This is the banana belt of Montana, with a lengthy dry-fly season that evokes jealousy from much of the rest of the Northwest. Dry-fly time begins in March with the hatch of skwala stoneflies on rivers like the Bitterroot and Clark Fork. Skwalas are the first large stoneflies of the season, and are olive-brown in colour, about size 10. Like most stoneflies, skwalas provide fishing for actively rising trout when the hatch is heavy, but also the opportunity for successful prospecting when the hatch is sparse. Stimulator-type dry flies with appropriate variations in size and colour, with or without optional features like egg sacs, rubber legs, and synthetic wings, nicely imitate the skwala and all our stonefly friends.

Next up, bug-wise, is the big cheese of western stoneflies, the salmonfly (*Pteronarcys*). You could easily spend a month river-hopping to stay on top of this hatch. The best-known salmonfly destinations might be the Madison in Montana, the Deschutes in Oregon or the Crowsnest in Alberta, but there are localized hatches on many streams in areas where the combination of fast, clean water and a rocky bottom occurs. These are the biggest of the common trout-bugs, and to imitate them our patterns should be tied in size 4 or 6 with a salmon-orange body. The hatch begins in late May at lower latitudes and lower elevations, and in late June or early July at higher latitudes and elevations. Hatching progresses up the river a mile or two each day and lasts a week or so in a particular area. You can catch fish on dries anytime after the main burst of hatching has occurred, but the best dry-fly fishing is often a few days to a few weeks later, when the adults return to the water to lay eggs. The bad news about salmonfly hatches is that they often occur during spring runoff, when dry-fly hopes are quashed by high and dirty water.

The companion bug to the salmonfly is the slightly smaller golden stone (*Perlidae*), which shares similar habitat. Though something of a lesser light in fly-fishing literature, the golden occurs in more streams, and often hatches in more angler-friendly water conditions a couple of weeks after both the salmonfly hatch and runoff.

While we're talking stoneflies, there is another one that has become popular with fly fishers recently. It's often referred to as a golden stone, because its size and general appearance are similar. But this bug is *Classennia sabulosa,* and its behaviour is different from the true golden stone's. Almost all hatching and egg-laying activity occurs after dark, and it is sometimes called the night stone for this reason. It's also sometimes called the short-winged stone because the adult males have short, half-developed wings. Unless you fish in the dark, you'll rarely encounter the adults, but you'll know of their presence by the vacated nymphal shucks that remain on riverside rocks. If you see a lot of these shucks, turn over some dry rocks near the water and you'll probably find the adults, which shun sunlight and will scurry to hide under other rocks. To fish this hatch you can stay out after dark, either dead-drifting or swinging dries, or you can start early in the morning before sun is on the water to take advantage of fish that have moved into the shallows to feed on egg-laying adults through the night. This hatch has become especially popular on Alberta's Bow River over the last decade or so, where it occurs from early July to mid-August, but you'll also find it on other large rivers throughout the West, including the Yellowstone, Colorado and Gunnison.

This takes us to the season of the drakes. The western green drake and the brown drake are among fly fishingdom's largest mayflies and provide some of the best dry-fly fishing of the summer. Green drakes hatch in the afternoons from either weedy or gravelly streams. They are around from several weeks to a couple of months because the hatch is usually comprised of two species – the big one (*Drunella grandis*) and the little one (*Drunella flavilinea*) – the latter called *flavs* by hep fly fishers. The most famous western green drake hatches occur on the Harriman Ranch section of Idaho's Henry's Fork of the Snake in mid-June, and the Frying Pan tailwater in Colorado in July, but these bugs are widely distributed, occurring in high-elevation cutthroat streams as well as more placid, weedy waters throughout Montana, Idaho, Colorado, Alberta and British Columbia. The best fishing is with imitations of the duns, but Mike Lawson reports that good fishing to green drake spinner-falls sometimes occurs early in the morning, which probably explains why most western fly fishers miss it.

Brown drakes (*Ephemera simulans*) are found in fewer streams and are around for a much briefer time than the green drakes, but provide extremely good fishing where they occur, such as on Idaho's Silver Creek and the Gibbon River in Yellowstone Park. They are found only in streams with slow water and silty bottoms, and emerge late in the day or after dark. Brown drake emergences and spinner-falls often occur together, so you'll need both some upright-winged duns and some spent-winged spinner patterns. The duns of both green and brown drakes can be imitated with Mike Lawson's Paradrake patterns in sizes 10 and 12, and the spinners are matched nicely with appropriately coloured Hen Spinners in the same sizes.

The third of the western drakes is the gray drake (*Siphlonurus*), which is a late-summer hatch on streams with slow water and abundant weed growth, like Oregon's Williamson River. What the gray drake lacks in widespread distribution it makes up in intensity and importance in streams where it exists. Because gray drake nymphs crawl out of the water onto bankside vegetation to emerge, trout rarely see the duns, but you'll need to carry some dark grey Hen Spinners in size 10 and 12 to fish the spinner-fall.

Late summer and early fall is grasshopper season throughout most of the West, but in truth it's hard to tell when stonefly season ends and grasshopper season begins. Golden or short-winged stonefly hatches overlap with the beginning of grasshopper time, and in late July it's hard to know what the trout think your size 8, yellowy-brown, down-winged dry fly is before they eat it. But all you need to know is that from that time through early October, such flies work from the Rockies of British Columbia to the perfect streams of Yellowstone Park and beyond. If you're serious about hopper fishing, you'll probably seek meadow streams such as the Yellowstone or Gibbon River in Yellowstone Park, or the Shoshone in the dry sage country near Cody, Wyoming. The best hopper fishing comes on warm days in sections of stream where there is good holding water near the shore and where the breeze blows from the bank to the water. But if all these requirements aren't in place, don't worry about it. Fish a hopper anyway because the trout don't know the rules.

I've been told that hoppers are killed by the first frost of autumn, but my observations suggest that it takes more than one frost to get them. Watch the weather reports, and if the nights stay relatively warm, you'll find hoppers into October. Fish will also eat hopper patterns for a week or so after the real ones are gone, because the recognition has been established.

I'm probably supposed to tell you which hopper pattern is the best, but I'm going to cop out and say I don't have a favourite. The new foam and rubber patterns are very effective, though there are really two categories of flies here. In one group are those carefully designed to represent a particular insect, like the Morrish Hopper, and their identity is readily apparent when the fly is in your hand. In the other group are flies that look nothing like any insect at all, and in fact seem to have been designed that way intentionally, possibly to demonstrate how ridiculous a bug a trout will actually take. Some of these have rattling eyeballs, a dozen rubber legs, and fluorescent, glow-in-the-dark wings. I know they work but there's something about them that offends my sensibility on behalf of the trout. But, suit yourself; the fish eat them.

Autumn brings one last big bug. The fall or October caddis (*Dicosmoecus*) hatches on many western streams in September and October, and though they are generally sparse in number, their large size (size 6 or 8), pumpkin orange colour, and proclivity for flying around in plain view make them noticeable. I can't say I've ever fished for trout that were actively feeding on October caddis, but I know that an orange Stimulator in size 6 works well in the fall at times.

So pick up a couple of extra spools of 3X and 4X tippet and start planning your season. You're going to save a lot of time on fly changes.

REQUIEM FOR HATCH MATCHING (2020)

First things first: what follows is presented with tongue at least partly in cheek. I know it's going to make me look like a curmudgeon who's stuck in the past, longing wistfully for the good old days, a Statler in search of Waldorf (google them if you have to). And after careful consideration I've decided that I'm okay with that if you are. But, a warning: I'm going to generalize some, maybe a lot. We all know generalizing is bad. I don't care.

In the – *ahem* – good old days, fly fishing was a game played with a certain objective, a more or less standard methodology, and a subtle set of unwritten rules (I hereby eschew the word *code*) – the three in combination establishing fly-fishing convention. Because the premise of the sport is (or at least was) to imitate fish's natural food items with our artificial flies, things play out best when we find fish that clearly are eating something. Since this all began with trout, and trout like to eat insects, that something is usually some kind of bug. And when the bugs are numerous enough, the fish eat them at the surface of the water where fly fishers can see it happening. Cue the dry-fly fishing. This sequence was for many fly fishers the defining encounter and challenge of our sport: *I see that the fish is eating something on the surface so I'll try to catch him by using an imitation of what he's eating.*

For a long time this was considered the pinnacle of the fly-fishing aesthetic, thanks perhaps to early writers who espoused and promoted it in North America: Theodore Gordon, Art Flick, Vince Marinaro, Doug Swisher and Carl Richards, and of course Ernest Schwiebert, who coined, or at least chose, the phrase *matching the hatch* for his first book title.

Fair enough; fast forward to today. Dry-fly fishing is still popular, but you don't have to look too closely to see that it's often quite a different type of dry-fly fishing. Fly fishers still seem to enjoy knowing what's hatching, and they still buy or tie dainty little emergers, duns and spinners to imitate the current hatch before heading to the water. But it's my impression, confirmed by observation, that oftentimes these flies never leave the safe haven of their new owners' fly boxes. Instead of using the imitative flies to fool fish that are feeding on the surface, many fly fishers turn instead to prospecting with large and sometimes ridiculous-looking dry flies. In many places where the rubber meets the road, it's really a case of the rubber meeting the water: "What'd ya catch 'em on?" "Big foam bugs, man! That's all you need for this river." Then it's home to quickly post a fishing report on social media (if it wasn't already done streamside): "Had a great day today on Stony Creek. BWOs hatching like crazy and fish rising everywhere. Slayed 'em on size 6 Chernobyl Ants and Club Sandwiches."

Is the big-foam-fly trend dominant everywhere? No, but I warned you I was going to generalize. To be fair, streams like the Henry's Fork of the Snake, Silver Creek and others are still bastions of hatch matching. Some big western rivers like the Missouri and Bighorn, though, are especially interesting. The hatches are heavy and rising fish abundant at the right times, and nearby fly shops stock great quantities of delicate bugs to match those hatches. And you will see a few fly fishers on foot, walking the banks or wading the flats slowly, hunting for and finding rising fish, then casting to them with tiny pieces of fluff tied to 5x fluorocarbon. But for every one of these there are five drift boats working mid-river with nymphs and big indicators, or nymphs beneath big foam bugs. Hatch matching seems to be fading, even in places where it could flourish.

Fly fishers like big foam flies because: (a) they're easy to see; (b) they're practically unsinkable; (c) they don't require fine tippets; and (d) they work. Prospecting with them is easier than finding, stalking and approaching a rising trout. How can all this be bad? My problem is that many of the flies look like they've been tied just to prove that a trout will eat a fly that looks nothing like a real food item. Should I care about this? Probably not. Do I care? It seems so. I wonder about the collateral damage this trend might be causing to the anglers. Effectiveness often comes with some casualties. There's less incentive to learn about trout-entomology and fish habits, there's less need to learn to cast well. And perhaps the biggest: when one method is used to the exclusion of others it can stall a person's development in the sport.

Let's consider the fly-tying part of the equation. I believe that the quest for more imitative flies is what drove people like Schwiebert, Swisher and Richards and René Harrop to learn about the creatures that fish eat, the way these creatures appear to the fish and the way they behave in each stage of their lives. These people weren't trying to find successful flies through random trial and error. Obsessed folks like Charles Brooks and Gary LaFontaine took extreme measures by going underwater with wet suits and snorkels to see what the fish's food looks like from down there, and to observe the way the fish respond to it. They wanted to learn, and this was one way they did. This process spurred the creation of patterns like LaFontaine's Emergent Sparkle Pupa, Brooks's "in-the-round" nymphs, and the first trailing-shuck dry flies and emergers. Curiosity and observation have always been cornerstones of the fly-fishing process, and this kind of thinking makes them the natural progenitors of fly tying.

Having said all this, is it not possible to use foam, jiggly rubber legs and sparkly synthetic materials to create highly imitative flies? Of course it is, as evidenced by beautiful patterns like the Morrish Hopper and various dainty ant and beetle imitations. Do these more imitative flies work better than a Club Sandwich? Maybe, maybe not, but that's not my point. My point, if I really have one, is that more imitative flies *should* work better and I wish it were so. If it were, it would validate the foundational principles of fly fishing. I don't like the idea of taking advantage of the fact that trout are sometimes embarrassingly gullible.

Am I saying we shouldn't use flies that don't specifically imitate something fish eat? Am I saying that I shouldn't do it, that I don't do it? No, I'm not. Am I being hypocritical? No, of course not... well, maybe just a little. Is fishing a big foam bug any different than throwing a Royal Wulff, you say? Because neither of them imitate a real bug, you say? Uh, let me think about that a minute. Hey, is it getting a little warm in here?

One of my favourite thoughts about fly fishing is that we don't do it because it's easy; we do it because it's not. This idea that once seemed noble now comes off as mostly snobbish. But it does seem that today catching the fish is de facto more important than *how* we catch the fish.

I could be wrong about the significance of hatch matching in our sport. I suppose it's possible – whether I like it or not – that it was simply a 50-year or so trend, a relic of the 20th century that was born, grew and is dying.

Maybe it boils down to this: I feel better using a fly that is intentionally created to imitate something. Is it okay to catch a fish with a stupid-looking fly? Of course it is; I just don't think we should take quite as much pride in it as we sometimes do. I'll paraphrase Norman Maclean here, who in *A River Runs Through It* said, "If our father had had his say, nobody who did not know how to catch a fish would be allowed to disgrace a fish by catching him." I'd make a slight change: "You should not be able to catch a creature as smart as a trout on a fly as stupid as a Purple Quad Wing Triple Decker Club Sandwich."

But you can. Thank God for René Harrop and Dave Whitlock.

WHEN SHOULD I CHANGE FLIES? (2021)

Regarding this question, fly fishers seem to fall into one of two categories – those who change flies more often than they need to, and those who don't change flies as often as they should.

In some ways a fly change is an over-overrated and over-overused response to rejection from creatures with tiny brains: I'm not gettin' any bites; must be using the wrong fly. If I was cynical (which of course I'm not), I might suggest that assuming the fly is the problem is a way of off-loading responsibility – a piscatorial version of the clumsy worker blaming his tools. But as I said, I'm not cynical.

Of course the fly could be the problem, but before you change it you should be as sure as you can be that that is indeed the case. For there are lots of other things that can be wrong, and if one of them is wrong, there isn't a fly anywhere that can fix it.

Once it becomes clear that the fish aren't going to eat what you're throwing, it's time to change something. In fact the question of when to change flies is really just that: a question of when to change something. The worst thing you can do when you're not catching fish is to keep doing what isn't working. Yet people do it all the time, hoping, I suppose, that the fish will eventually feel pity.

The first thing to consider is whether the fly is going to the right place. Make it easy for the fish to eat your fly. Don't ask a fish to move a few feet to eat if you can ask it to move just a few inches. This, of course, rests with your casting.

Once you've made a perfect cast you have to get perfect behaviour from the fly. If it's a dry fly, it has to drift without drag while it's in the fish's view. If it's a nymph, it has to get close to the bottom and then drift without drag. If it's a streamer, it has to behave like a baitfish when it's in the fish's view.

Meeting these objectives might require changes in casting position or terminal tackle. It doesn't matter how many casts it takes, you shouldn't consider changing the fly until you know you've made perfect shots several times. (And by several I mean five or ten times, not 250 times.)

A critical factor that's not given enough consideration is the leader. It should be long enough to prevent the fish from being alarmed by the fly line landing nearby, and the tippet should be the right diameter for the fly (for trout fishing divide the hook size by four to get the "X" diameter of tippet you need).

The sport's quintessential confrontation comes when a fly fisher encounters a trout rising steadily and frequently in moving water. You know where the fish is; you know that it's feeding. So you try to determine which stage of which insect it's eating, then stand in a place where it's easy or at least possible to get an accurate cast followed by a perfectly drag-free drift right over the fish (not three or four feet off to the side of the fish). Sometimes a steadily rising trout will stop rising for the few seconds it takes for your fly to drift over it, but gets back to business as soon as your fly is out of view. While this kind of behaviour drives me crazy, I also kind of admire it. It's a sure sign that the trout is looking but not buying, and that's a sure sign it's time to change something. You might try a longer leader or finer tippet – or a different fly. You could switch to a slightly different imitation of the insect the fish is eating, or to an emerger or spinner. As long as the fish continues to feed, you're still in the game.

But if the fish stops rising altogether, stop casting immediately and watch awhile to see if it resumes. If it does, carry on casting to it. If it doesn't, you've probably spooked that fish. Make a couple of Hail Mary casts and then move on.

When we see trout rising we possess extremely valuable information, and this is our preferred scenario. In these situations fly changes can come fairly quickly because the fish's response will be readily apparent. But more often we're "fishing blind" and it's a little harder to be sure we've put the fly in exactly the right spot, so fly changes will come a little more slowly.

When you're fishing unsuccessfully in a good spot there's a decision to be made. You can stay there, ratchet up your determination and persevere in the belief that the fish are there and you'll eventually get 'em if you try enough flies and methods. But another response that qualifies as "changing something" is changing location. Sometimes moving a couple of steps one way or the other will allow you to get a better drift. Or you could move to the next pool, or to a different type of water. As a last resort you can get in your vehicle and drive to a different stream.

But if you do that you're admitting defeat. As long as you're okay with that...

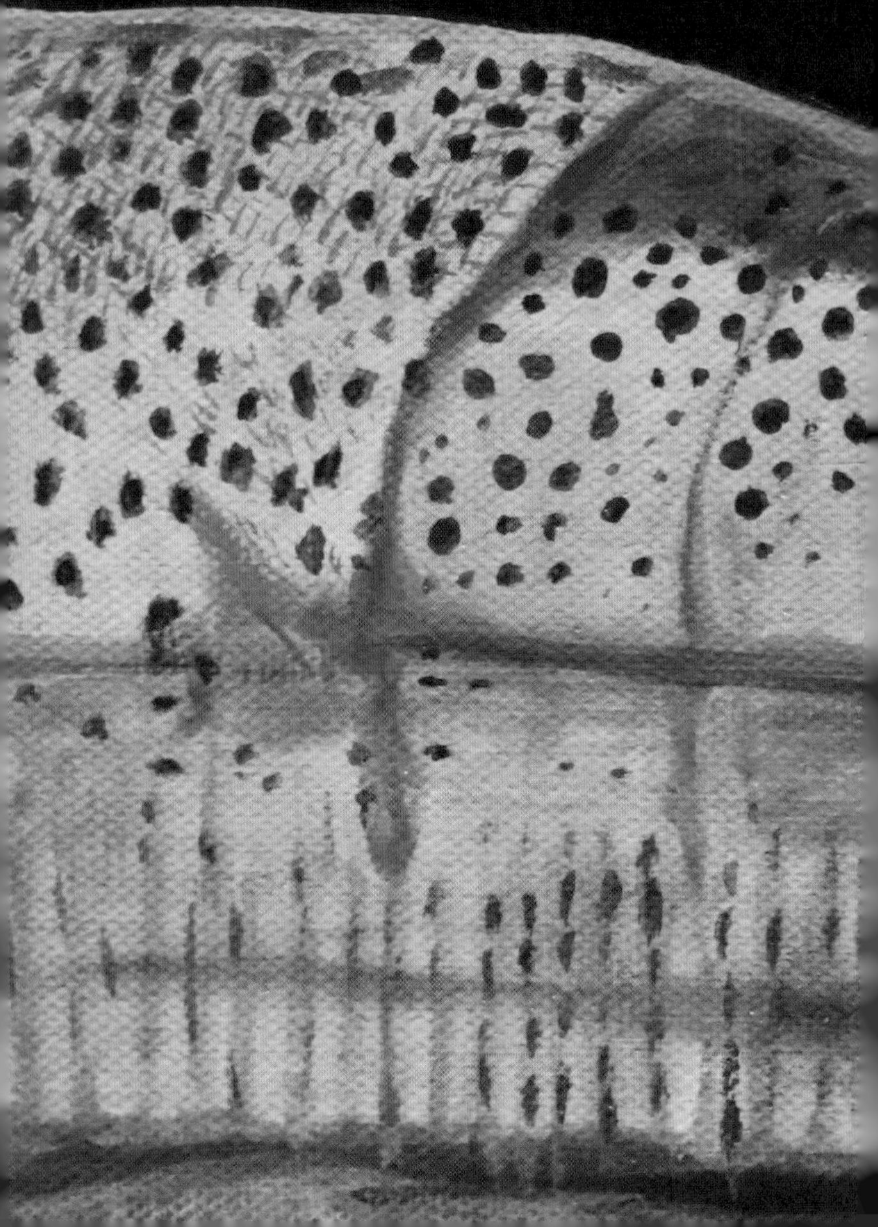

3. How

WHEN CUTTHROATS GET THE BLUES (2014)

That's such a good title for this story that I'm using it even though it's clearly a borrowed – okay, a *stolen* idea. So the obligatory apologies go first to author Tom Robbins, who wrote a novel called *Even Cowgirls Get the Blues,* and songwriter Rodney Crowell, who wrote a song of the same title. Then fly fishing's literary spokesman, John Gierach, saw the charm and titled one of his books *Even Brook Trout Get the Blues.*

With all that out of the way, let me tell you what the title means. Cutthroat trout are perhaps the most beloved of western trout, primarily because of their penchant for feeding on the surface. They come to the top for a well-presented dry fly more willingly, reliably and frequently than other trout like rainbows and browns. But what nobody seems to be saying is that cutthroats aren't always so co-operative, and can become very difficult to catch by September. After they've spent a few weeks getting poked with the odd hook, they get to the stage where they've "had enough" and become very careful about what they eat. I don't know if this qualifies as "getting the blues," but they're good learners and it's my belief that an "experienced" cutthroat is as hard to fool as the most sophisticated rainbows and browns.

Cutthroats seem to start the summer fishing seasons a little on the naive side. Maybe they have short memories, for after a long winter with no fly fishers pestering them, they react "properly" to the first arrival of aquatic insects, and as long as the water is warm enough, they rise nicely to natural insects and surface imitations when they get the opportunity. They seem especially fond of big dry flies that imitate stoneflies and large mayflies. This tendency is well documented and pontificated upon by fly fishers throughout western North America. "Cutthroats live at high elevations, in harsh, cold-water environments where the hatches are sparse, so they have learned to feed whenever there's something available to eat. Blah, blah, blah..." You can find this kind of information in magazines, books (including mine), and all over the Internet. That's because it's mostly true.

Everybody – even new fly fishers – seems to know about and take advantage of this trait, and cutthroats are great dispensers of confidence to rookie anglers and are frequently the inspiration behind flowery prose in magazines and books from angling writers.

But things change in late summer. If most fly fishers were honest (like that's ever going to happen), they'd admit that a size 10 Stimulator with a Prince Nymph dangling beneath it works for a while but becomes less effective as the season goes on. The formerly "dumb cutthroats" are now extremely difficult to fool.

My favourite example of this behaviour came when a very experienced angler/friend and I could do nothing – *nothing* – with a pod of big cutthroats plainly and eagerly scoffing western green drake mayflies. That was a decade or so ago, but it's happened again numerous times since, always late in the season, usually in September. In the fall of 2013 another experienced friend and I had our clocks cleaned by steadily rising cutthroats on a rocky western stream. My companion finally caught one, but only after he'd made at least a half dozen fly changes, reduced his tippet to 6x and used a downstream presentation with some kind of obscure micro-emerger.

This behaviour from cutthroats comes along often enough to make me say that if you haven't seen it, you haven't fished for them enough. Keep at it and you too will find occasions when you want to tear your hair out.

So what to do about it? Here's where it will start to sound like I know something about this, but trust me, even though these are my best "tricks," they only work *part* of the time when the cutthroats get snooty. So these are suggestions, not guarantees, and when these ideas fail you, you're on your own.

First, get rid of the big flies, unless you see that the fish really are eating big flies. Second, try to forget for the time being that you're fishing for cutthroats. Treat them as you would the most selective, hard-fished brown trout. If the fish are rising, try and find out what real bug they're eating. In late summer or fall it's likely to be something small, like a blue-winged olive mayfly, an ant, or a midge, so pick a small fly from your box. And choose a sparsely tied imitation, because cutthroats, like all tough, selective trout, seem more likely to accept something sparse over something prickly with gobs of hair, hackle and rubber legs sticking out everywhere. Those are early-season cutthroat flies.

Then, fish carefully, the way you would to the most experienced and paranoid trout. Err on the small side with your tippet, even going down to 6x. Cutts are not particularly strong fighters, and if you're careful you can land most of the biggest ones on light tippet. Be sure that you get a completely drag-free drift, and if necessary and possible, position yourself upstream of the rising trout and use an upstream reach cast so the fly drifts over the fish before the tippet and leader do. If you make completely drag-free deliveries to a rising fish from this position without success, you can assume the problem is your fly. So then you can begin the fly-changing routine, using different imitations of different stages of the bug you think the fish is eating. Eventually, the fish may make a mistake and take your fly. When this happens you'll think you've got it figured out, and you have – for that fish. When you find another rising fish, you might have to start the process all over again, because the fish seem to become more individualistic as the season goes on. One might eat a blue-winged olive emerger and the next one might have nothing to do with it.

If the fish aren't rising, you still have a good chance to catch some on dry flies. You can fish with an imitation of the last insect the fish have been actively feeding on, which you can determine with a visit or call to the nearest fly shop. Or you can fish with terrestrials. While other creatures may fall into the terrestrial category, that section of my fly box contains mainly hoppers, ants and beetles. In many ways a hopper makes the most sense, as it's the biggest item and the one that provides the fish with the most protein for its effort. But experience shows that cutthroats often prefer the smaller terrestrials. I've learned this by fishing two dry flies simultaneously – a good-sized hopper and a much smaller ant or beetle about a foot away on a dropper. This offers the fish a choice of two contrasting flies, and the hopper lets me know the approximate location of the small fly, which I probably can't see. It's amazing how often the fish, which undoubtedly sees both flies, opts for the small one. It's been suggested that the big fly gets the fish's attention, but because the fish has been hooked on big flies previously, it's now shy of them and takes the small, "safer" fly instead. That's attributing a lot of reasoning to a fish, and I'm really not sure if I buy that theory. So I don't know why fish do this; it just seems that *small* and *sparse* are the watchwords when choosing flies for tough, late-season cutthroats.

It's common to find cutthroats rising sporadically rather than steadily. When I encounter this I assume the fish are feeding occasionally on the surface, but frequently on nymphs beneath. Something that has worked for me in this situation is fishing a size 16 or 18 nymph in the area where the fish has been rising. It's hard to beat a Beadhead Pheasant Tail for this. I use a small piece of buoyant yarn (commercially available as "strike indicator yarn") about two feet above the fly as an indicator, because the yarn lands gently and doesn't spook fish. Don't use a Ping-Pong ball–sized indicator and a size 4 San Juan Worm for this, as it will spook the fish immediately. I always try a few dries over these occasional risers first, but rarely give up on one without trying a small nymph.

Of course you can also fish a small nymph "blind" if you like, working it through the places you know cutthroats live – the deeper green holes, the slow troughs along fallen trees, the undercut grassy banks. Your friends might chastise you for fishing nymphs for cutties, but that's just something you'll have to live with.

There are still days in late season when the cutthroats behave like – well, like cutthroats, and eat huge, rubber-legged foam flies, but sooner or later you'll find some that have "got the blues" and just won't eat those flies. They're dumb cutthroats no more.

ON THE CONTRARY... (2020)

Our sport's deepest thinkers have made better thinkers of us all. Perhaps the best and deepest was the late Gary LaFontaine. He was never satisfied with status quo or doing something a certain way just because that's the way we've always done it. He asked if the way we've always done it makes sense, or if there might be a better way. An exploration of his books (*The Dry Fly: New Angles, Trout Flies: Proven Patterns, Caddisflies* and others) will convince you of this. One of the things he questioned was our assumptions about how trout see and respond to their food. So of course he put on diving gear, lay quietly on the bottom of a trout stream and watched the bugs and the trout. Then he came up with better imitations and methods of fishing them. To him, contrary thinking and innovation were simply a logical way of doing business, and we're better and further ahead because of what he learned and shared with us.

When it comes to contrary thinking and innovation, a few unusual flies and methods have (pardon the expression) emerged recently. Along with these are some that I believe to be still gestating and in the pre-emergence stage.

The now-seemingly fundamental idea of dry-fly fishing was an innovation itself in its early days, but once established it was done almost entirely in an upstream direction in moving water. This was to achieve the all-important drag-free drift, which is still required to adequately imitate the way most adult insects behave when they're on the surface of the water. On some of the UK's revered chalk streams anglers are still required to fish dry flies upstream only.

Thanks to circumstances and that all-important maternal motivator, *necessity*, in the 1970s or so some radical, revolutionary and clever North Americans found that in certain situations a dry fly could be delivered (and also accepted) more successfully when presented with an across-and-downstream cast. Heresy? Not quite, but at the time unconventional for sure. Details are not warranted here, but the gist is that when properly presented down and across, with the correct reach cast (or reach mend), the drift is drag-free, but with the added benefit that the fly arrives in the fish's view before the leader does. This is not something that's important everywhere, but it's very important and beneficial in some places, most specifically streams with slow, flat, clear water and PhD trout.

While we're talking about the direction we fish, let's consider streamers. They've most often been fished with a relatively simple down-and-across swing to which rod-tip movement and a stripping retrieve is added. This lets the fly mimic both the motion and direction of the little fish that streamers are intended to imitate. And it works fine – except when it doesn't.

The times it doesn't are when the layout of the banks and stream doesn't allow them to be fished that way, or when the trout are being trout and simply don't respond to it. What's needed are some additional ways to present streamers. In tiny, bush-lined streams, down-and-across is impossible so the only option is to cast upstream and retrieve the fly back toward you. The best retrieve is just slightly faster than the speed of the current, which allows a weighted streamer to reach good depth easily and make its way down the current toward you with a tempting up-and-down jigging action.

Casting a streamer upstream is also an excellent way to fish near undercut banks, fallen trees and other bankside cover. A conventional down-and-across cast might place the streamer near the productive cover initially, but once the retrieve begins the fly immediately moves away from the cover into open water that a trout might be reluctant to enter. An up-and-across cast keeps the fly closer to the cover longer.

My longtime friend and outdoor mentor, the late Bob Scammell, had an interesting way of fishing in caddisfly season. He used three flies on his leader: a weighted larva imitation on the bottom, a pupa in the middle and a buoyant adult pattern at the top. He'd adjust things so the larva would reach the greatest depth, the pupa would be just beneath the surface, and the dry would be at the surface. You could fish this in either an upstream or downstream direction, but I believe Bob fished it mainly downstream. A cast quartering down, followed by a couple of quick upstream mends, allows both the larva and the pupa to sink, with the larva going deepest. On the swing the pupa rises to the surface in a nice emerging motion. All the while the dry caddis alternately drifts and hops on the current with each mend or movement of the fly line, nicely mimicking an egg-laying adult. Is this clever? I think so.

What about flies and fly patterns? Terrestrial fishing is in vogue these days, primarily – in the West at least – because that's the category into which grasshopper fishing falls. In eastern North America and elsewhere in the world, other land-borne bugs are considered as important as grasshoppers are in the West. Beetles, ants, cicadas, caterpillars and other terrestrial bugs are regularly imitated in other places. My fishing pals from Pennsylvania used to tell me (as long as nobody else was in earshot) about fishing inchworm patterns on the tree-lined stretches of the Yellow Breeches and other PA streams. They were also fans of ant and beetle patterns. They fished all of these terrestrial bugs as dry flies, as most of us do, but they also fished sunken versions of them. Turns out that land-based insects float, but not forever. A sunken beetle or ant (or inch-worm) pattern can work very well. I'm trusting that I'm not in trouble for spilling the beans here, but in my defence I've kept this under my hat for at least 20 years. Another dip into the Gary LaFontaine library reveals that he fished with – you guessed it – sunken hopper patterns. What a surprise.

There are a couple of flies I've found a need for but haven't been clever enough to devise on my own. So in true McLennan fashion I'm happy to explain the problems but too lazy to find the solutions. And so I put these out here, in hopes of spurring action from fly tiers. First, I need a true dry/streamer hybrid. This is a fly that floats on the surface and imitates a large, longish insect like a stonefly or hopper, but sinks slightly and "transforms" into a streamer with a slight pull on the line. It needs to be carefully constructed with materials that are buoyant, but not too buoyant. It might need some type of collar or "spoiler" to send it beneath the water when the line tugs on it (see the Dahlberg Diver pattern). And it should have a soft "wing" (marabou, ram's wool?) to give it the enticing, slithering motion of a streamer after the fly has sunk.

Why not just fish dries and streamers separately, you say? You can, except in one situation. It's nearly impossible to fish a streamer close enough to really gnarly structure like root balls, undercut banks, log jams or any place with a lot of snaggy cover. But you can fish a dry fly quite nicely in these places because you can let the fly drift in, watching it all the way, and remove it just before it gets into trouble with the snags. Often the current causes the dry fly to "bounce" off the snags without hanging up. But what if the trout won't eat a dry? It would be nice to be able to show them a streamer, but in those places it's very difficult. Because the fly sinks immediately and most of the time you can't see it, it drifts, sinks and snags if you let it get too close. With the hybrid I'm craving, you could let the fly drift in very close to the snags, and whenever you want you could tug on it so it drops beneath the surface and then you could retrieve it as a streamer. Think about it: dead-drift on the surface toward bushes, up against roots or along a log jam, and if nobody eats it on the surface, fish it out as a streamer. Bob Scammell had some prototypes of this type of fly that he called Jekyll and Hyde, but I foolishly lost the samples he gave me, so I'm left with nothing but his good idea.

How many times have you had a big trout (think brown trout and bull trout especially) come charging out of nowhere to take a run at a six-incher you're dragging in to release? When this happens to me I do what I've been told: cut back the leader, put on a streamer, throw it out there where the attempted mugging occurred and try to make it behave like the struggling little fish. Sure, but that almost never works. I'm convinced that's because the movement imparted by stripping a conventional streamer doesn't come close to replicating the panicky struggling behaviour of a little fish that's attached to a hook and line. The fly-fishing world needs a streamer that better imitates the movement of a small fish that's hooked on a line and is fighting to get away. For an imitation to behave suitably it might have to be tied so it comes in diagonally when it's retrieved, so that the more you pull on the line, the more the fly resists coming in and tries to move perpendicular to your pull. In the spin-fishing world there are plenty of plugs that behave like this, so surely it's possible with a fly. Maybe if there was a way to attach the leader partway down the hook shank?

So here's an appeal to all you tiers out there: Remember that things that are weird and wacky today might be routine tomorrow. So put away the foam for a few minutes, do us a favour and create some of these new flies. You can send the prototypes to me.

MEMORY AND SELECTIVITY (2020)

One day many years ago when I was working in a fly shop I heard a tale of fantastic fishing for big trout on dry flies. The fellow was leaning on the display counter and holding forth while customers wandered about. Bugs were thick on the water, he said, fish were rising everywhere, he said, and of course he had the right fly and was dialled and hauling 'em in steady. Because such stories are not unusual in a fly shop, and because I had heard so many of them, as soon as this one began I immediately engaged my default defence mechanism and pretended to be astounded one more time. I don't recall whether my internal voice was calling BS or whether I was jealous, wishing I could experience such fishing someday, but I was brought to a jarring halt when the teller of the tale turned toward me, put his hand up to invite a high-five and said, "That was a great day, wasn't it, Jim?" "Huh?" I said. "You mean I was there?" When I thought hard I was able to remember the day, but not the way he remembered it. Maybe he caught all the fish.

But that's the way it works, isn't it? Memories in general, and fly-fishing memories in particular, are based on exaggeration and selective recall – which upon reflection is a beautiful combination. It makes memories of an event better than the event really was, and the loftiness of the memories increases in direct proportion to the time elapsed since the event. I suspect this is somehow beneficial.

It's not that we don't have poor trips; we just forget about them or disregard them altogether. My second trip to New Zealand, for example. It got off to a bad start when our flight to LA was delayed by fog in Calgary, causing us to miss our connection and arrive on the South Island a day later than planned. After that the trip was a near washout because of rain and high water, which can and does come in NZ, and as a result I don't remember much about it.

On my first BC steelhead trip I caught one on a dry fly 20 minutes into the first day, and finished the trip with 16 fish in 8 days. I know this is true because my partner kept a diary. On my second trip a couple of years later he also kept a diary. It says I caught one fish in four days, but I don't really remember.

Or how about a doomed bird-hunting trip to Saskatchewan with two partners about ten years ago? Shortly after our arrival a "weather bomb" of unseasonable and ridiculous wind, cold and snow settled on us and kept us indoors for the entire four days. All I recall is that we drank coffee and other liquids, watched western movies and took naps. No gun barrels were soiled and no birds were harmed in the making of this story.

Another example of how our outdoor selectivity works is reflected in the outdoor media, where written words, still-photography and video transport people into someone else's experiences, portraying these experiences more or less as memories. Having a couple of times been involved in outdoor – uh – deception, via the medium of television, I'm qualified to speak here. When the programs aired there were always a few people who objected if an episode showed great fishing and a lot of fish. They said things like, "But it wasn't real. It was a TV show. They had the best guides, and were on the best water at the best time. Of course they caught piles of fish." My response was always, "But who would watch a fishing show with lousy fishing? How much casting and banal streamside banter can you stand?" Eventually I realized that some of these people were the same ones who complained if there weren't *enough* fish caught. "It was boring. They didn't catch many fish. They had the best guides, were on the best water at the best time, but all they did was sit on the bank and talk philosophy because they couldn't catch anything."

There's a certain reverence for the past that seems to permeate our sport. My first trip to New Zealand was in 1989, and at that time many fly fishers believed that the fishing there was in serious decline and was nothing like it had been in the good old days of 30 or so years previous. Yet if you inquire today, there's a good chance you'll hear something like this: "Well, it's not as good as it used to be. It's gotten crowded and there's not as many fish. Thirty years ago it was really something." See what I mean?

Someone once described fishing as large periods of complete boredom punctuated by very brief periods of intense excitement. Thankfully our memories disregard the former, while collecting, retaining and exaggerating the latter. I'm pretty confident this trend will continue and am sure that in a couple of decades my kids and grandkids will look back longingly to the early 21st century, when the fishing and hunting were still really good and hadn't been ruined yet.

ON BEING A NOTICER (2011)

What's the most valuable asset a fly fisher can have? Is it one of the physical skills – the ability to cast accurately or far, perhaps? Is it a scholarly knowledge of aquatic insects? Is it an intimate familiarity with the habits of the fish?

As important as technique and knowledge are, I submit that it's the broader, more embryonic trait of *curiosity*. Curiosity is what makes us first wonder what's going on under the water, and then understand that what's going on under the water is connected inextricably to what's going on above and around the water. Curiosity is what makes us accept and embrace the fact that every answer to a fly-fishing problem arrives with a brand new set of questions.

This realization came to me slowly, primarily through the influence of other fly fishers who were further along the curiosity continuum than I was.

When I was working in a fly shop, a guy came in to shoot the breeze one summer day. "How's your fishing been?" I asked, using the shopkeeper's standard opening line.

“It’s been really good,” he said. “I noticed tons of ladybugs in my yard and along the river this summer, and I wondered if the fish ever ate them. Well, they do. I pumped a couple of trout’s stomachs and they were full of them, so I worked out a little ladybug imitation and it’s been doing great.” When I thought about this I recalled seeing far more ladybugs than usual too, both on the river and around home. But what I didn’t do was wonder if it meant anything to the fish. Ladybugs aren’t on the usual menu of trout food, according to the trouty books, so it never occurred to me to consider them. In my defence, I wasn’t alone here; this fisherman was the only one who even mentioned the ladybug proliferation that summer. And I’ve never seen such numbers of these bugs since.

Then there’s the whole “San Juan Worm” saga. By the mid-1980s I was aware that significant numbers of aquatic worms live in the weeds and silt of my home river, the Bow. I found them when sampling the stream bottom looking for the mayflies, stoneflies and caddisflies that all my entomology books told me I should find. I found the insects I expected, but I also found a lot of little aquatic worms. But again, what I didn’t do was wonder if it meant anything to the fish. Wouldn’t one of the books have said so if it did? What I should have done was create an imitation and try it out. It would have worked, I’m sure, and for once I would have been ahead of the curve – fishing an aquatic worm imitation long before anybody else, and before the San Juan Worm pattern migrated from its New Mexico birthplace to become the standard it now is on so many western rivers.

One of the most curious fly fishers I know is John Randolph, longtime publisher and editor of *Fly Fisherman* magazine. He came to Alberta to fish with me for a few days a number of years ago, and when he arrived I found that he had studied our area and its natural and human history prior to his trip. He wanted to know – and found out – what made our economy tick, what all of our best trout streams were and what fish lived in them. This research had not been a chore; he simply couldn't help himself. The greatest example of his insatiable curiosity came the day he, another friend and I stopped at a restaurant for breakfast in rural Alberta. When we were done, one of us paid the bill, one or two of us paid a visit to the men's room and then we met at the truck. Or at least two of us met at the truck; there was no sign of John. Eventually we found him back in the restaurant, now seated at a table with a group of local ranchers, holding his own in a deep discussion about calving season, cattle prices and pasture condition. As you'd expect, his curious nature serves John well in most of his endeavours, including fly fishing.

Two other fly fishers possessing the "curiosity gene" were Charles E. Brooks and Gary LaFontaine, both from Montana, and both now deceased. They also simply couldn't help themselves. Both felt the need to know what goes on under the water, and both chose to find out by donning snorkels and masks and observing trout behaviour from the bottom of the stream. They reported their findings in their books: Lafontaine's *The Dry Fly: New Angles,* and *Trout Flies: Proven Patterns*; and Brooks's *The Trout and the Stream*.

One of fly fishing's perfect virtues is the way it both rewards and encourages curiosity. Those already in possession of a curious nature can't help but use it in their fishing. Those who don't have it see how beneficial it can be, and work to develop it.

So here's my advice for someone who knows the theoretical and practical sides of fly fishing but is still hungry to improve: Become a *wonderer* (not a *wanderer*, though I guess that's okay too), and a *noticer*. If you wonder and notice when you're on the water, both your success and your enjoyment will increase, for curiosity is the godfather of understanding.

DEGREES OF DIFFICULTY (2016)

Is fly fishing difficult? I guess in some ways it is. And I guess in some ways that's kind of the point.

In any type of individual sport, because there's no opposing team or player (at least not one comprised of humans) there are certain "impediments to success" that we accept as part of the endeavour. This is probably not too far off a reasonable definition of "sport" or "fair chase." A certain amount of acceptable difficulty is at the core of what we do. This is true of other activities, including hunting, mountain climbing and even golf (there are easier ways to get a little ball into a hole in the ground, but that wouldn't be playing golf, would it?).

We're fortunate in fishing that the fish are neither impossible to catch, nor catchable with every one of our attempts. Success that comes too easily or too often contradicts the definition of sport and taints or eliminates any sense of satisfaction. That's why trying to catch a trout with a size 20 dry fly on 6X tippet is sport (or *sporting*), while throwing a stick of dynamite into the water is not. Remember the old story of a fanatical fisherman who dies, and in the afterlife finds himself catching increasingly larger fish on each successive cast? In case you've missed that story, the man starts out enjoying this, but soon realizes he's not in heaven, but hell.

Philosophical navel gazing aside, in fly fishing there's a delicate balance between a degree of difficulty that we can live with and a degree of difficulty that makes success impossible. And because our desire to participate largely rides on the *possibility of success* (dismissing for a moment the worthy attraction of simply being outdoors in a nice place), when that possibility disappears, the likelihood of enjoyment disappears also.

Maybe some examples from both ends of this spectrum will have value. In New Zealand most of the stream fishing is "sight fishing." You walk the streambank with the bright sun behind you, looking into the water trying to spot a fish before casting. It's done this way because there are low numbers of fish in the streams and because the water is clear enough that an experienced eye can see some of the fish. It's not easy, but it can be done – part of the time. It's an acceptable degree of difficulty. But if you're trying this on an overcast day when the surface of the water is nothing but glare, it's pretty much hopeless. You can't see into the water at all, and that's an unacceptable degree of difficulty. You'll probably find something else to do that day.

One challenge I enjoy is fishing to rising trout that are very difficult to fool. This occurs most often in heavily fished spring creeks and tailwater streams. There are prolific insect hatches in these places and the trout get very selective to both fly pattern and presentation, and fly fishers must do everything they can think of to try and tip the scales their way and fool the occasional fish. Sometimes the fish win and I go away shaking my head. I'm okay with that. Other times I fool a few fish and feel good about it. I'm okay with that too. But either way it's an acceptable (to me) degree of difficulty. The fish are there, they are visibly feeding, so I should be able to catch them, but I may or may not be able to do so.

There are days when I'm in such a place and the bugs are hatching the way they're supposed to, but for some reason the fish aren't rising. Yes, I know, they're probably feeding heartily on nymphs beneath the surface and I could probably catch a bunch by fishing nymphs. But because I'm a snob about these things, I don't want to fish nymphs here. If they aren't rising, I'm taking my bugs and going home.

Recently Lynda and I fished a favourite tailwater river with another couple, hoping for lots of opportunity to cast to rising trout. The first morning we decided to try a favourite section of flat water where there were plenty of fish feeding last year. We parked the car and got all rigged up – flies sorted, waders on, lunch figured out, sunscreen applied – and headed for the river. When we first got out of the vehicle we noticed an odd but vaguely familiar odour. Something had died nearby, but not too recently. When we got to the place where we crawl under the fence that runs beside the railroad track we saw the source of the stench. A dead deer was lying precisely in the only crawl-space under the fence. Whether it died right there or was placed there shortly after its death by a clever but devious angler to discourage other anglers is uncertain. What was certain was that we weren't dragging it out of the way. It was definitely an impediment to success. That was the only route we knew to the water we wanted to fish, so we spent the day looking for other places. As it turned out, the fish weren't rising much in the other places, and of course we don't know what happened on the lovely flat just beyond the stinky dead deer. We thought we had everything covered, but sometimes difficulties arise that you have no chance of anticipating or overcoming. Life – and fishing – is not always fair. But then, we don't do it because it's easy; we do it because it isn't.

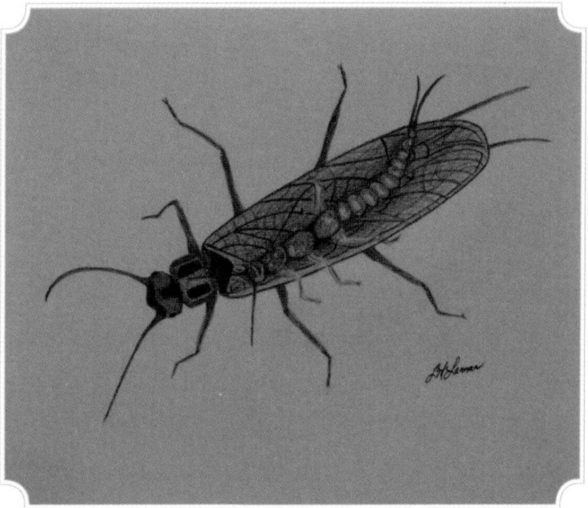

FAIR WEATHER FISHERMEN? (2014)

Since fly fishing is an outdoor sport, we're inclined to care about what the weather is like when we do it. And from a strategy viewpoint there are legitimate considerations about the ways weather affects our fishing. Some fishing, such as cutthroat fishing near the mountains, or saltwater fishing in the tropics, is best in warm, sunny, calm weather. But as much as we appreciate this pleasant co-operation between Mother Nature and the fish, it doesn't always work that way.

Certain types of bad weather can make for good fishing. Rainbow trout, brown trout, steelhead and other species are frequently most active – and as a result most readily caught – when the weather is less than perfect for humans. Experienced fly fishers know that on many streams the *Baetis* genera of mayflies, called blue-winged olives, provides the best dry-fly fishing of the year. The BWO fishing is at its best when the weather is not. Cool, cloudy, damp days bring out both the flies and the trout, and as a result there's an odd irony to this hatch. Fly fishers flock to streams like the Missouri and Henry's Fork, hoping for the rising-fish dry-fly fishing that makes these rivers famous. If the weather is fair and bright, the river gets crowded and the fishing is disappointing. Yet if the weather turns damp, cold and nasty, the bugs and the trout appear in droves, but most of the fishermen disappear, opting to stay indoors or hang out at the fly shop and complain about the weather. Out on the water the trout are pigging out and the handful of guys who are braving the nasty weather – wearing fleece, rain jackets and gloves – are having the time of their lives.

That's what Lynda and I were hoping for when we left on a little late-September fishing vacation a few days ago. It was cold and rainy at home, and had been for weeks. The daytime highs hadn't reached 20°C since August. Water temperatures in our home streams near the mountains dropped into the 5°C range and the fish were behaving the way you'd expect them to in late October.

We didn't have a lot of time for this trip so we didn't go far, just a five-hour drive south into the next major river drainage. Because we're with-it, new-age fly fishers, we checked websites from several fly shops at our destination before we left home, and found that their weather had been similar to ours but slightly less severe, and that the BWO hatch had started nicely just a few days earlier. But when we arrived it was as if somebody had turned the calendar back two months. The day we travelled it was bright and clear and the high reached 30°C. We started fishing about noon the next day, just in time for a gale-force wind to kick up. Bright, sunny and windy doesn't sound like BWO weather, and it wasn't. We quit fishing in mid-afternoon and went back to town so we could hang out at the fly shop and complain about the weather. While we were there we checked the forecast and were disappointed to find that it called for more of the same. But wait a minute; the guys at the fly shop told us that there were still some tricos around each morning, and we saw reasonable numbers of caddis fluttering in the grass yesterday while we were on the water. So we figured the thing to do the next day was to hit the river in the morning when it was calm, then relax in the middle of the day when the wind and heat were worst, and fish again in the evening.

So we went with that strategy, feeling kind of smug about how clever we were. We got to the water about 9:00, saw just a few tricos and no rising fish. This was troubling because we knew the wind-clock was ticking. Sure enough, about noon the occasional morning zephyrs increased to flag-tearing velocity. But that's also when we started to see fish. Grasshoppers were active in the heat, and the wind was blowing from the perfect direction to deposit hundreds of them onto the water. The short version of the story is that we had a great afternoon of fishing in spite of, or actually because of, the wind and heat.

I know this is the way hopper fishing can be in the right circumstances, but the circumstances were right for something so different just 48 hours previous that it was almost inconceivable that we could have stumbled into this. I guess it's a reminder of two things we're already supposed to know: first, that weather and fishing conditions can change quickly, and second, we might think we're pretty clever, but we really have no idea what's actually going to happen.

So is there a lesson in here somewhere? Maybe. When it comes to planning we can look at the long-term averages for things like water level, air temperature and hatch dates, to get an idea of what to expect when we get to our destination, but we have to remember that an average is comprised of all sorts of highs and lows. If it's 20 degrees colder than normal today and 20 degrees warmer than normal next week, the average is going to look pretty much like it always does. So I guess we're back to just taking our best shot and living with what we get. That's how our averages are made too.

TIMING IS EVERYTHING (2010)

It occurred to me recently that almost everything about fly fishing is critically tied to timing. And if I can coin a couple of slightly ostentatious phrases in the process, I'll point out that this includes *macro-timing*, which is what you use when you're trying to meet a specific insect hatch, run of fish, or other significant piscatorial event; as well as *micro-timing*, which is what lies at the heart of good fly casting. In another context micro-timing is what's required when notifying a spouse or boss of a short-notice, yet-to-be announced fishing trip. It's a micro-timing error, for example, to make such an announcement on a day when you're late for a meeting or have neglected to complete an important domestic or professional task.

A fishing trip itself is rife with ways in which timing – good or bad – can influence a day on the water. Think about it. Have you ever returned home from a poor day only to talk to a friend who was on the same water the same day and had great fishing? This could be a matter of skill (not likely, of course) or dishonesty (some possibility), but more likely it's just timing. If he started before you did, or stayed after you quit, he might have been present for some feeding-fish activity that you missed. Some insect hatches are brief, and spurred by very specific weather conditions. In the West we like to brag about the great weather we usually get in the fall (perhaps first articulated by Ian Tyson in "Four Strong Winds"). But it's often when the weather is *bad* in the fall that dry-fly fishing is best. There is a short-lived afternoon blue-winged olive mayfly hatch that often brings fish out in a big way, but only if the weather is sketchy enough that you give some thought to staying indoors. Just last week a companion of mine was having trouble getting warm and dry after a soggy night in a tent, so he opted to call it a day about two in the afternoon. The fishing had been just fair up to that point. I stuck it out in the rain and cold and had some fine sport when the little flies showed up about an hour later.

Just so you don't think I'm always on the positive end of such transactions, I'll relate another example. On a cold and rainy day some friends and I finally stopped fishing in the belief that discretion is the better part of valour. We got back to camp and were quite comfortably into the après-fishing conversation and libations when the others in our group arrived a couple of hours later to report that when the rain finally did stop, a hatch of big mayflies came off for about an hour and the fishing was great. See? Timing.

What about when something good happens on one part of a lake or stream, but not another? Another after-fishing conversation this summer revealed the fact that the water I was on had an inspiring hatch of green drakes for a couple of hours, while the water just a few miles downstream did not. I didn't know this was going to happen and it was more good fortune than anything else, but it is an example of how a fishery operates with its own agenda and its own timing.

When the day of a long-awaited fishing trip finally arrives certain considerations have to be made that require proper timing. Generally this can be summarized by saying that the more people in the group, the earlier you should start the day, especially if it's important to be on a certain piece of water at a certain time. This is necessary because the more people there are, the more chance somebody will sleep in, the more chance somebody will need to stop along the way for a coffee or a bathroom, and the more chance somebody will have brought the wrong rod, or will need to stop at a fly shop on the way to the water.

Ever seen a truly superb fly caster at work? The kind that makes you stop what you're doing and just watch? The words used to describe these people's casting are usually *smooth,* or *effortless*. They cast in what almost seems to be slow motion. There's no extra force, no unnecessary motion, just polite little nudges of the fly rod at precisely the right moments. That, friends, is timing. And it's one of the reasons women often make great fly casters. They don't adopt the nearly universal male approach of hitting harder if something isn't working right. Women seem to sense that fly casting is a matter of timing rather than a matter of strength.

One last thought about timing: if you find a fish that's feeding, try and catch it immediately. I learned this the hard way in New Zealand many years ago when, after a tough morning, we finally spotted a nice brown feeding in a pool right where we had decided to stop and eat lunch. "Let's try for him after we eat," somebody said. Okay, fine, except when we looked for him after lunch he wasn't there. I know timing is an important element in comedy, but we didn't find this very funny.

4. Navel Gazing

BIG FISH, LITTLE FISH, ANY FISH (2014)

What would make for a perfect day of fishing? A lot of fish? A big fish? A lot of big fish? We all have something in mind when we slam the tailgate shut and start down the trail toward the water, and it's usually shaped by optimism. Nobody begins a day of fishing by saying, "I know this isn't going to work..." If you're returning to a familiar place, you're going there again partly because of the fishing you've had there in the past. If it's a new spot, you've probably done research that suggests you *should* have good fishing there. And though neither you nor your companion would ever say it out loud, you're both thinking the same thing: "Maybe this will be the day – *the* day – when everything that's supposed to happen happens in a big way. Maybe today fish will be rising all over the place, the wind won't blow, and I'll have the right fly." Does such optimism ever fully bloom? Not often, I'm afraid, but we do get glimpses and fragments of these kinds of days, and it's these that keep us planning trips and dreaming about fishing. And when a day on the water does tilt a little more than usual toward perfection there's probably a big fish or two involved. When it comes to fish, most people consider bigger to be better.

So just why is a big fish more desirable than an average fish? It's self-evident, isn't it? Average is... well, *average*, and though the dictionary's definition of the word isn't negative, its connotation is; most people equate average with mediocre. Who wants to be associated with anything mediocre? Who wants to catch a mediocre fish? Then there's the intellectual angle. It's safe to assume that a big fish is an older fish, an older fish is a smarter fish, and a smarter fish is more difficult to catch. Therefore it must take more skill and knowledge to catch a big fish than it does to catch a small or average fish. In other words it takes a smarter and better fisherman to catch a big fish. And don't we all want to be considered smarter and better?

All of which explains why I'm always a little suspicious of people who claim that they like little fish just as much as big fish. I run across this from time to time, usually from people who are interested in racking up numbers when they're on the water. When I hear of somebody catching an outrageous number of fish somewhere I assume the fish are all small, but maybe that's just my rationalization when I don't catch as many as other people do. "I could catch as many fish as you if I wanted to," I think, "but I'm not after a lot of fish; I'm after the *right* fish." Feel free to consider these the thoughts of an insecure snob.

When someone makes a statement about catching an extremely high number of fish I don't wonder about the truth of the statement (though perhaps I should); instead I wonder what the point is in catching that many fish. Did fish number 74 make the day better, or somehow prove something that fish number 73 didn't, or that fish number 36 didn't? I never count the fish I catch, preferring to judge a day by how I feel about it when it's over, although when things are tough it's hard not to know where you stand, numbers-wise. If the number is somewhere between zero and two, it's pretty hard to feign ignorance, even to yourself.

I think my wife has this part of the game figured out. Lynda fishes hard until she catches a couple of fish that she really wants (and in her case they are often big), then she stops fishing and concentrates on photography for the rest of the day. Her level of angling satisfaction is annoyingly high.

There are times when catching a big fish upsets the piscatorial apple cart. Ever catch a big one in a place where there aren't supposed to be any big ones? When this happens it seems like a gift from God. After all, if the place was attractive enough that you liked fishing there without the expectation of a big fish, it becomes something really special when a surprise lunker shows up. But be warned, this is a good news / bad news story. The good news is obvious: you've caught a big fish where you didn't think there would be one. The bad news is that your expectations have now been severely messed with, to the point where that which previously satisfied you on this water probably won't satisfy you from now on. You can file this under "Be careful what you wish for..."

A big fish can also be bad news if it shows up too early in a fisher's career. Many years ago Lynda and I took one of her young music students on a float on the Bow River. He was about 14, a pleasant young man, and had expressed an interest in fly fishing. He'd never held a fly rod before, so we did a quick casting lesson on the shore, then plopped him into our drift boat and pushed off. About 20 minutes later he said, "I think I've got one." Indeed he did have one, and when the dust settled another 20 minutes or so later we were photographing the little guy with a hog-jawed, two-foot-long brown trout. He, of course, had no idea what he'd just done, but did think that this fly-fishing stuff was pretty cool and that we should do it again sometime. Neither Lynda nor I had the heart to tell him that he should expect to fish for another decade or two before he caught another fish like that one. We've lost touch with this young man and I've often wondered whether that first fish improved or ruined his chances of becoming a fly fisher.

But what about small fish? Where do they fit into the picture? Are they a source of embarrassment, proof of only primary-level skill? If we put our egos aside, it's clear that small fish are important. They fill a crucial role from both a biological and human perspective. Biology-wise, all the big fish we like to catch start out as little fish, so every little one could be the seed of a dream. And under the mathematical principles embraced by Mother Nature, a bunch of little fish are required in order to produce just a few big fish.

From the human perspective, little fish serve a critical role because they're more co-operative when it comes to allowing themselves to be caught. Everybody needs to catch something fairly soon after they start trying, and that need is often fulfilled by small fish. New fly fishers, especially young ones, have no biases against small, naive fish. These little fish are often responsible for hooking newcomers on the sport, and this makes their role arguably more important than that of big fish.

Which brings us to the category of "any fish." This smacks, probably with some justification, of desperation. We've all said, or at least thought, "any fish is better than no fish." We usually think it late on a day when we're barrelling headlong toward a skunking. And when we say any fish, we really mean *any* fish – any fish, any species, any size. If it has fins and scales, it qualifies. Even non-sport fish make the cut on days like this, and it's interesting how a whitefish or sucker takes on a bit more shine when the trout aren't co-operating.

I've often thought that if fishing were great all the time, there would be little reason for doing it, and if it were terrible all the time there would be even less reason to do it. A crotchety old fly fisherman – who might have been me – once said that he'd never met a fish he didn't like. And while it could be argued that this sets the bar pretty low, it certainly helps make all fishing days good days.

EXPECTATIONS (2013)

The hope for what might happen on a fishing trip is really the driving wheel of the whole operation. You go somewhere because of what you hope you'll find – good conditions and abundant fish that are in a receptive mood when you cast your flies to them. But of course it doesn't always turn out the way you hope it will. Most of the time reality falls quite short of hope. How we handle or manage our expectations can have a surprisingly large impact on the pleasure we take from a fishing trip.

Expectations are the "elephant in the drift boat" for fishing guides. Every guide's dream is for their clients to arrive with realistic expectations of what the fishing will be like, based on the conditions of the moment and an accurate assessment of their own fishing skills. It's this last one that gets sticky. Ask a bunch of guides what skill they wish all their clients possessed, and the overwhelming answer would be "casting." "If a guy can cast, I can get him into fish" is the maxim of fly-fishing guides from Alaska to New Zealand. Knowing the skill level of the client in advance helps the guide plan a day and select a location that gives the angler the best chance of success. But the guide's conundrum is that he can't say straight out to a prospective client he's never met, "So, how well can you cast?" At that stage the guide is still in the business of making his only first impression, and this isn't the best way to do it. Even if he finds a way to surreptitiously ask the question, perhaps by couching it in a different question, like an inquiry about where the client has fished recently and how successful he was, the guide still doesn't really know whether he's going to have Lefty Kreh or Joe Btfsplk with him. That's because most experienced fly fishers believe they are good anglers and good casters, but in reality the majority are somewhere a little to one side or the other of "adequate."

And when a barely or less-than-adequate caster meets finicky fish, strong wind or other difficult conditions, expectations take a beating.

Still, expectations are the root of optimism, and optimism is something we can't do without when anticipating a fishing trip. There's no point going if you don't expect things to turn out well. But if conditions point to the likelihood of modest success, your expectations need to be dialled down a bit.

Overinflated expectations often come after a first trip to a new place gives you outstanding fishing. As great an experience as that is, it creates a precedent and sets the bar – often much too high – for the next trip to that place. We all know this, of course, but it's surprisingly difficult to adjust expectations downward. That little voice in our heads is insistent: "Remember what it was like the first time you fished here? It should be just as good this time."

Those who can temper their expectations, though, are rarely disappointed. It's like a concept from the business world, which says it's best to underpromise and overdeliver, rather than the reverse. If you can apply that to your fishing trips you'll be prepared for the fishing to be a little less than you hope for. And it's always a better trip when the fishing exceeds expectations rather than falls short of them.

My strongest memory of expectations that were too high is from a trip I took to New Zealand many years ago. I had been there before and had had a taste of how good it could be, so my expectations were sky-high. However, this second trip was plagued with weather issues. New Zealand is a place where it can rain. And rain. And rain. And it did. Every morning I'd raise the curtain in the bedroom of the lodge, hoping to be blinded by bright sun and blue sky, conditions that not only preclude rain but also provide the best circumstances for seeing fish, which is the first step in catching a New Zealand fish. But every morning the sky was grey, dark and drizzly. The streams were dirty, the guides were discouraged, and the fishing, in short, was pretty much a bust.

Did I learn anything from this trip? I'm not sure I did. Our expectations can be pretty resilient. Because we subconsciously view our first trip to a place as the rule, rather than the exception to the rule, I pretty much wrote off the second trip, when the conditions and fishing were poor, as an aberration.

I did make another trip to New Zealand a couple of years later, and this one was the best of the three. Of course in my mind this proved that the second trip was just a glitch. So if I go there again, I'll do what everybody does – I'll expect perfect weather, windless days and more big fish than I deserve.

But that's just optimism, isn't it?

HEALING AND COPING (2018)

People sometimes describe the fly-fishing experience as "spiritual" in nature. And though this seems a common notion, I don't agree. Fly fishing is fascinating, fun, absorbing, puzzling, satisfying, intriguing, exhilarating (and exasperating), but – to me, at least – not spiritual.

During a recent long winter I viewed a number of the latest fly-fishing films. I was pleased to notice what seems to be a trend away from the simple chronicling of young, hip, fly-fishing bums doing their thing in exotic, expensive places for audiences that wonder who funds such capers and how a person can get in good with them. There are now fine films being produced that use fly fishing to tell strong and moving stories. This started with *A River Runs Through It*, I suppose, but the difference is that that movie was made for a general audience. The best fly-fishing films today are made for us – the insiders, the people who already "get" fly fishing. As a result, the understanding of the power and strength of fly fishing's attraction needn't be articulated, and this allows an extremely strong connection to be drawn between the storyline and fly fishing, as long as the story rings true.

Some of the best films use the healing power of fly fishing as the principal storyline. One such film deals with a Second World War veteran who returned to France and a place of bad memories – but this time to fish there. Another is about Montana guides who teach fly fishing to injured veterans who've returned from Afghanistan and Iraq.

These are the dramatic stories, but it's not too hard to find people who have experienced the healing power of fly fishing, albeit in ways that probably won't wind up on film. After making a presentation about fly fishing at a downtown library once, I was approached by a homeless man who had come to hear my talk. He engaged me in a short conversation, and the point he wanted to make was, "Fly fishing saved me." He lived downtown near the river, and spent as much time fishing as he could. Religious connotations aside, I think his statement meant that he found purpose and something to do – and something to anticipate doing – which was helpful in his struggle.

Fly fishing can help us through many difficulties, primarily by demanding and taking all the participant's attention, thereby diverting the mind – at least temporarily – away from negative or painful things and directing it toward positive and pleasant things. When someone experiences this for the first time, our sport becomes the gateway to a corridor of new and healthy fascination.

A big part of fly fishing's ability to help us cope comes from the way we anticipate a planned outing. An upcoming fishing trip gives us something to focus on that is positive, and whatever difficult things that must be dealt with first are somehow softened by the knowledge that fishing waits afterward: "I'm not looking forward to that unpleasant business meeting on Friday, but I know I'll be on the water on Saturday." Without something to help us look beyond the difficulties, the difficulties are – well, more difficult.

Sometimes fly fishing simply takes us to places where healing from other sources can occur – places we wouldn't find ourselves in were it not for fly fishing. This, I suppose, is the "generic" benefit of being outdoors in nature. That benefit can be delivered by many different outdoor activities, but sometimes fly fishing is what gets troubled people outdoors.

There are people around who take the greatest satisfaction through helping others. This applies to more than just fly fishing, but it does apply to fly fishing. Some people – like my wife – are simply wired this way. Lynda derives more satisfaction and sense of worth from helping someone else catch a fish than by catching one herself. This can serve as a healing or coping mechanism for her, and I suspect many guides find it true for themselves if they look deep enough.

In *A River Runs Through It,* fly fishing wasn't enough to save Norman Maclean's brother Paul, who ultimately succumbed to forces stronger than himself or fly fishing. But when he was on the water, he was happy, he was a fine fisherman, and in the words of his Presbyterian-minister father, "He was beautiful."

Maybe that's the therapeutic benefit that fly fishing brings – some help in coping with our struggles. And if that's the best it gives us, it's enough.

CONNECTIONS (2015)

In October, Derek Bird and I, along with a film crew, were in British Columbia shooting programs for *Fly Fusion* TV. We were fishing small streams that come from the Cariboo Mountains and flow into Quesnel Lake, a large glacial lake in north central BC.

In the fall, sockeye salmon that have spent two or three years in the Pacific Ocean make their way up the Fraser system, through Quesnel Lake and into these small tributaries to spawn. The resident rainbow trout in the lake follow the salmon to eat the eggs. We were there to fish for the rainbows.

As we fished, Derek and I were both struck by the mystery of the way the trout were drawn to these streams. We wondered how they knew when and where to come, and marvelled at the way their lives are directly and crucially tied to the lives of the salmon. Grizzly bears and bald eagles were on the same streams eating the dead and dying salmon, and their presence made us aware of the connections that existed between them and the sockeye. It's not hard to extrapolate further still, and come up with other connections – between the salmon and the ocean, between the ocean and the rivers, between rivers and glaciers, between forests and clean water.

One of these days provided one of my most vivid of fly-fishing memories. I was casting a couple of hundred yards or so downstream of Derek and the film crew. One of them shouted to get my attention, and then pointed. A hundred metres downstream of me were three grizzly bears, busy on the far bank, looking into the water, clambering about on the deadfall along the shore. They were fishing too, and were completely oblivious to what I was doing. Fishing took a backseat to this spectacle, which I'd never seen before. In most of humans' encounters with wild animals, the animals are well aware of us, and their behaviour is determined almost completely by our presence. But here I was watching magnificent wild creatures doing exactly what they do when we're not around. This, I realized, is rare.

It's also easy to find the connections between these things and people like Derek and me – two more creatures drawn to this place at this time by the presence of the salmon.

This theme is not new, and was perhaps understood first and best by Indigenous People, but is articulated beautifully in a book by a Wisconsin farmer, Aldo Leopold, called *A Sand County Almanac.* Published in 1949, it is considered a seminal and foundational work in the North American conservation movement. It expands on a premise frequently attributed to John Muir, a paraphrase of which says, "When one tugs at a single thing in nature he finds it attached to the rest of the world."

An important lesson this, and one brought to vivid life in the wilderness of BC in October.

ROAD TRIPS (2015)

No matter how good the fishing is near home, we're all fascinated with the idea of going somewhere else to do it. Even if it's a long drive, if you can get there and back in one day it's not really a road trip. And if it's a business trip or a trip to visit family or non-fishing friends during which you hope to sneak in some time on the water, that's not really a fishing road trip either. In my book, for it to be a bona fide fly-fishing road trip it requires an overnight stay of a few days, and the priority must be on the fishing. All details must be chosen and executed to maximize the fishing experience.

Maybe we have such affection for fishing road trips because of this simplicity of objective and the fact that we can't put this much priority on fishing when we do it near home. When the fishing is close to home we often have to squeeze a day or part of a day in among all the other things that life requires. When it's a road trip for the sole purpose of fishing, the focus is squarely on the prospects for fun. And the peripheral components of such a trip – who you go with, where you stay, where and what you eat – are a big part of the fun and the memories the trip creates.

There are at least a couple of different categories of fly-fishing road trips. There are those to new places and those to places you've visited before. A trip to a new place brings a distinct type of excitement. There is research to be done, decisions to be made about where and when you go, tackle to be organized, flies to be tied. These trips can be made with companions who've been to the destination before, or they can be to destinations that are new for everyone.

If you're returning to a place, it's undoubtedly because you had a good experience there in the past. And after you've gone to the same place with the same people a couple of years running it may become an annual trip, which to me is a separate category and the best kind of road trip. These eventually take a priority position on the participants' calendars and all that's left to be determined is, "When are we going this year?"

There's also the "trip of a lifetime," where you save money, do tons of research and prepare for years to go someplace you've dreamed about. It might turn out to be a one-off experience, or it might be so good you simply have to find a way to go back, even if it requires waiting a few years again.

There are different ways of setting up road trips. They can be camping trips, staying-with-friends trips, motel trips or high-end lodge trips. There may or may not be guides involved. I once heard about some well-heeled fly fishers who decided they should do a three-week trip to New Zealand with only one stipulation: that there be no budget. That meant that whatever struck their fancy was in play – hiring helicopters to get to remote streams, using guides, staying at fancy lodges, dragging a supply of high-quality wine with them, staying at upscale hotels if they were handy. I never heard if they did it, and though I'd certainly be jealous of such an adventure, I take a bit of sour-grapes satisfaction in knowing that even this kind of trip can still go off the rails.

I've had some great fly-fishing road trips, most of them with Lynda. Our most recent one was not particularly exotic, but it was a good one. We have long-time friends who spend the last week of September every year fishing in BC. It's prime dry-fly time for cutthroats and for years Lynda and I have politely listened to their stories, watched their videos of the trips and reluctantly declined their invitations to join them. But last year we just said, "We're coming," and found a way to clear the calendar. It was a time of low pressure and high pleasure. No need to start fishing early, no need to stay on the water til dark. Though they don't live there, our friends own a condo in a town near the fishing, so we all stayed there, cooked some of our favourite meals together and laughed a lot. We're going to do it again.

So do fishing road trips rate higher on the enjoyment scale than fishing favourite waters near home? I don't think I'd go that far. For many of us, the engine that drives fly fishing is anticipation, and water both near and distant produces a good amount of it. So excuse me if I seem greedy, but I want both. I propose a double toast: to fly-fishing road trips, *and* to fishing near home.

TECHNOLOGY VS. TRADITION (2016)

Like almost everything, fly fishing has changed and is changing. Once perceived as an eccentric old sport that was either difficult to learn or was *portrayed* as difficult to learn by its stuffy, tweed-wearing, pipe-smoking practitioners, fly fishing is now being taken up by a growing group of young, enthusiastic devotees who've decided the sport is cool. But that doesn't cover it. Many of these young fly fishers are extremely knowledgeable, and perhaps more importantly, are coming into it from a background of environmental appreciation, unlike many of my era who had to be educated on this matter after the fact.

Today's young fly fishers bring with them an understanding of the technology they've grown up with, and that makes some of us older fly fishers nervous, for tradition and technology make strange bedfellows. Once we old guys get comfortable with the term "social media" (as Orvis board chairman Leigh Perkins told me, "I can't explain a lot about social media, but I'm sure it's important"), we'll realize that it is, among other things, a tool with which to communicate fly-fishing information. That's good – I think. But perhaps not always. It gets a little sticky right about here. Are social media, the Internet and technology in general helping fly fishing or harming it? I'm pretty sure they're helping fly fishers by making the sport more accessible and easier to learn. But what about things like Google Earth? Many fly fishers use it to get a bird's eye view (or a satellite's eye view) of potential new fishing spots. Is this "cheating?" Probably not; it's kind of like using a really advanced topographical map. What about using camera-equipped drones to check out the water before making the walk to see it in "real life?" This gives me a little more pause for thought, but how much different is this from looking up stream-flow information on the Internet to determine if a river is at a good level before making a long drive?

Or what about checking online fishing reports, taking into account the possibility, remote as it is (hah!), of exaggerated, inaccurate or blatantly misleading information? And to open an especially stinky can of worms, what about *posting* online fishing reports – especially reports of exceptional fishing that reveal exact locations? At this point the devil on my left shoulder, who represents my cynical, old-fashioned side, says, "Are these people nuts? Do they really want a few dozen new fishing partners standing in the best pools the next time they visit that stream? It wasn't like this in the old days." The angel on my right shoulder, representing my kinder, gentler side, says, "Now hold on a minute. If a lake or stream is going to have an ongoing and growing group of protectors, it needs people who are passionate about fishing it. The greatest protectors of fish and wildlife have always been fishers and hunters who care about the creatures they pursue and the places the creatures live. So it's not wrong to make it easy for people to find good fishing."

There are other types of collisions between technology and tradition. A couple of fly fishers go to a lot of trouble and hike a long distance into a remote backcountry stream. They've done their homework and are packing fishing gear, camping gear and food for a few days of exploring and fishing in the middle of nowhere. After a strenuous hike, they arrive at the stream just in time to see a helicopter land and deposit four eager fly fishers and their guide on the gravel bar just ahead of them. Sounds like a bad deal for the hikers, doesn't it? But what if the chopper is carrying fly fishers who can't physically make the hike? Are they villains because they can afford the means to overcome that handicap?

I've begun to wonder how important it should be to make fly fishing easy. In some cases I think it's quite important, because, as my harp-playing friend has explained, fisheries need fishers, some of whom in turn need the benefit of certain technologies to allow them to enjoy fly fishing – either to get started in it more easily or to enjoy it safely in the face of increased age or physical limitations.

But is there a chance we occasionally come close to making it too easy? The traditions of fly fishing, some of which mainly celebrate the difficulty of the sport, are important to me and I worry a little that some of them are being pushed aside or are slowly disappearing.

But what really is a tradition? It might be simply doing something the way we grew up doing it. Several years ago my daughter was drifting the local river with some friends and called me from the river on her cell phone. I heard her voice tremble as she said, "I just caught the biggest brown I've ever seen!" I was thrilled with the news, but it was definitely a new way of receiving it.

I suspect technology is helping create new traditions – like phoning somebody from the stream after you catch a big fish, or taking a photo of it and putting it up on social media while you're still on the water. I'd never think of doing either of these things, and they certainly aren't traditions for me, but they may be for the latest crop of fly fishers.

Perhaps in my case the trick is to use technology to allow me to continue to participate and enjoy fly fishing, but not to let it compromise or diminish the traditions that I consider to be important.

I'll have to work on that.

WHY DO WE DO IT? (2020)

Is it just me?

Fly fishing has a lot to attract people to it: beautiful settings, physical and mental benefits, interesting problems to solve. But we can experience these things other ways in the outdoors, so why do we need to do it in places where fish live? More specifically, why do we have to *catch* those fish? Am I the only one who's stumbled across this question and feels a bit uncomfortable about it?

I'm not saying I don't want to catch them or that you and I shouldn't try to catch them. I'm not preaching to anyone here. And this isn't about whether or not fish feel pain. I'm squarely in the camp with people who participate in this sport, enjoy it and believe it's good for us and ultimately good for the fish. But I do wonder why it isn't enough just to know about the fish, to watch them and be happy they're there. Why do we have to catch them?

I've read about the practice of using flies with hook points removed so we can do everything but – well, catch the fish.

Fishing but not catching – sort of – except doing so intentionally. This, it's said, allows us to partake in all the elements of fly fishing – stalking, observing, casting, eliciting a strike – without poking the fish in the mouth with a sharp piece of metal. While I sort of understand this, I'm not sure I could do it. I'm afraid it would allow too much potential for regret. What if the biggest fish of my life took a hookless fly? For the vast majority of us, fishing includes catching and touching the fish, or at least getting a close look at them once they're close enough to touch.

As evidence of how far this obsession can go, I present the following example: In a previous century I hosted a fly-fishing TV show called *Iron Blue Fly Fishing*. We shot an episode with my daughter, who was 12 at the time. Prior to the shoot I scouted some locations, looking for a place that was accessible for all of us – camera guy, director, daughter and me – that was pretty and gave us a good chance at some fish. We made the show without revealing the location, and in my humble opinion it turned out well, with Deanna catching a number of fish, including one exceptional specimen that of course we used at the climax of the episode. A number of years later – ten, maybe – I ran into an acquaintance who brought this show up in conversation. When no one else was around he leaned toward me and quietly said, "I figured out where you filmed that episode with your daughter, you know…" It turned out he was right, although before we confirmed that he was correct there was some careful jockeying for position as to who was going to say the stream's name first (if he named a stream first, but was wrong, he would be giving me some of his secret information, you see, and if I named the stream first – well, you get the idea).

Once we'd established that, yes, he did know where we had made that show, I asked him how he'd figured it out. He explained that he had recorded the episode on his VCR (this was well before smart-TV days), and taken still photographs of his screen when the show was playing on his TV. He printed the photos and kept them in his vehicle. Then he went exploring. There were mountains around the stream so he had a general idea of where to look. He checked out all the streams he found that were about the right size, comparing the streams, the mountains and the backgrounds with those in the photographs, one by one eliminating possible candidates. And eventually – I don't know how long it took – it worked, and he knew where we had been. I was floored that he had gone to all this trouble to find out where some guy and his little girl had had good fishing once. I don't know how many hours, miles and dollars he expended on this undertaking, but if this isn't obsession I don't know what is.

While I thought this behaviour was well over the top, part of me admired his perseverance and dedication to the task, odd as the task itself seemed. And to his further credit, though I had seen him many times between the airing of the show and his revelation to me about his successful search, he never once asked me where the stream was.

This is extreme, but who doesn't feel jealous and want to "be there" when photos and videos of big fish show up on social media? Don't we all take an initial quick glance at the fish and then examine the surroundings slowly and carefully to see if there are any hints about location?

So though it seems it would be nobler to take the high road and declare that I'm glad there are fish around, and am perfectly satisfied just knowing they're there – that would be mostly horse feathers.

So why isn't it good enough just to know about them and be happy they're there?

I don't know, but it just isn't.

TO SHARE OR NOT TO SHARE (2010)

Fly fishing is widely regarded as a sport rooted in tradition and guided by etiquette, but there are some grey areas surrounding the question of whether a person should share (or how and to whom to share) good fishing spots with others. Those committed to our sport and concerned with its future believe that if it is to continue to exist it needs a constant crop of new, enthusiastic and hopefully young fly fishers. This belief makes the more experienced anglers want to help out the less experienced ones who are trying to get started. After all, somebody probably shared a few spots with us when we were new to the game, and if it wasn't for them maybe we'd be playing golf instead of fishing. That's the noble view, and it's easy to believe it and preach it until you walk a couple of miles to a secret beaver pond and find a group of five fishermen already there, led by the guy who learned about the spot from you just a few weeks ago. Your altruistic sense of benevolence fades a little at this point.

If somebody shows you a good spot, he may ask you to agree not to return to it unless you're alone or with him. This arrangement works quite well, but there are still some odd situations that can arise. For instance, after a few years you might find that several people have taken you to the same "secret" spot. This happens to me occasionally, and I always get nervous when I'm at such a spot with one of the people who took me there, planning what I'm going to say if one of the other people happens to show up, and wondering if there's any chance he'll believe me.

Here's another problem. Somebody you fish with infrequently takes you to his secret spot and it's great. You can't wait to go back, and finally the next season you're able to schedule a return, by yourself as per the agreement. Then a couple of days before the Saturday of the trip, your best fishing partner calls to ask if you're available to go fishing on Saturday. Now what? Your choices aren't great. You can lie to your best fishing buddy and tell him you're busy that day, and then sneak off to the secret spot; you can break the agreement and take him there; or you can fish with him, but not at the place you really want to fish.

On the other side of the coin there's the pre-emptive, passive-aggressive approach, which says it's better to show a good spot to a friend than to keep it secret from him, because if you show it to him and make him agree to the rules, you retain control over what he does with the spot. This tactic is best used when the friend is keen and curious and you suspect that he may find the spot on his own, in which case you would lose control over what he does with it or who he shows it to.

These questions and conundrums (conundra?) have existed for a long time, but our friend the Internet has made it even more complicated. It's one more way to share or reveal great fishing spots, not just to the guys in your local fishing club, but to the whole fly-fishing world. This is, to say the least, a contentious topic. Just check any fly-fishing bulletin board to see how frequently and quickly any discussion about "hot-spotting" deteriorates into name calling and worse. And how long until some enterprising Internet-marketing fly fisher runs an ad on a fly-fishing website, offering GPS co-ordinates for great spots? I can see it already. There will be photos of big fish, some sleazy music and a seductive voice that says, "For the co-ordinates of a location with 16- to 20-inch rainbows, send $59.95. For the co-ordinates of a location with 18- to 22-inch rainbows, send $79.95. Please add $20 for brown trout locations."

A fly-fishing guide was feeling particularly magnanimous one day and suggested to two friends that they try a place where he had had terrific fishing a week earlier. The two friends went there and had one of the best days of the season. A few days later the guide who made the suggestion called to find out how they had done because he had some clients teed up and he wanted to take them there if the fishing was still good. Now here was a dilemma. Calling up the ghost of Ed Zern, who wrote, "Fishermen are born honest, but they get over it," the beneficiary of the guide's generosity said, "The fishing was terrible. We think you were putting us on." File this under "All's fair in love, war, and fly fishing."

I know a fly fisher who came upon another prickly situation. He had great fishing somewhere and emailed photographs of the huge fish to some of his friends and fishing partners, coyly neglecting to say where the photos had been taken. Most of his buddies knew what he was up to and didn't want to allow him the pleasure of refusing to reveal the location, so they didn't ask about it. But one fishing partner who was accustomed to special privileges did ask. But our hero was steadfast, holding firm to the cause of secrecy, and refused to say where he'd been. Just because it was his mother didn't mean he could bend the rules.

TINY PERFECT MOMENTS (2012)

This past season I found myself alone on a river on a dreary fall afternoon. I had expected to spend the day with a fishing partner, but circumstances intervened and it turned out to be just me, the river and blue-winged olives. I didn't want to fish nymphs or streamers this day, so I went looking for rising fish.

Eventually I found one right against the bank, back under an overhanging bush – a good rainbow tipping up elegantly to take one of the drab little duns every 30 seconds or so. I could see the white of its open mouth each time it fed, and sometimes its tail would tick the surface from underneath or wave in the air slightly as the fish nosed back down after eating. I've always considered these the signs of an especially content fish. It was well back under the bush, but a couple of feet upstream of him was a small opening where I'd have to drop the fly. I was standing across from the fish and had to make a longer cast than I wanted to because deep water prevented me from wading closer. I worked at it quite a while, making maybe 50 casts without ever getting one in there far enough. And, with plenty of real flies drifting right over, there was no reason for the fish to move out a couple of feet to take mine. But at least it kept rising, which told me it was still in the game. Then, for some reason – probably because whatever breeze there was let up for a couple of seconds at exactly the right moment – a cast turned over perfectly. The fly landed in the gap upstream of the fish and started to drift on the current, and I knew that if the fish didn't take on this cast it wouldn't be taking at all. Then the fish rose and ate my fly in the same gentle way it had been taking the naturals. I fought and landed it – a good fish, though neither its size nor fight was especially noteworthy. It was just a good fish from a good river. But *everything* was noteworthy about the way its capture occurred. I remembered this fish and the cast that fooled it fondly through the rest of the day and indeed the rest of the week, and it's probably my favourite fishy memory from last season. But if a non-angler had been watching the whole event, his comment, or at least his unspoken thought would probably have been, "It sure took you a long time to catch him, and he's not even that big."

The truth hurts sometimes, doesn't it? And it's true that most of our fishing is made up of long periods of pleasant but somewhat mundane and unexciting activity, punctuated by infrequent moments of extreme excitement. But that's the difference between an angler and a non-angler. The angler gets this and accepts it; the non-angler never will – unless he undergoes a conversion.

You can spend a whole season seeking one of these brief, perfect moments if you're a steelhead angler. And you can spend a whole career chasing one if your quarry is something like a permit or a trophy bighorn sheep. I had a long conversation with a dedicated sheep hunter in a fly shop once. He had been hunting them for many years and had never shot one. He was not disappointed by this, even though he had spent significant money on trips and gear, and significant time learning the habits of his quarry and honing his shooting skills. There had been many opportunities to shoot good rams, but he had never pulled the trigger. When I prodded him further, he explained why. "I think that if I ever shoot a ram, I'll have to quit hunting them," he said. "And I don't want to quit hunting them."

What makes these kinds of hunting and fishing endeavours *sporting* is the fact that when you decide to participate, you accept the guarantee of an inherent low success rate. In an odd way, this is precisely why such activities are attractive. Success is priceless largely because it is infrequent.

It's easy to observe this principle in other parts of life also, like the arts, for instance. Jazz musicians search for the perfect improvisation, the moment when it seems roles have been reversed and the instrument is now playing the player. When that happens, everybody in the band knows it and everybody in the audience knows it. But it doesn't happen on every tune; indeed it doesn't happen on every gig.

I was sitting at home one summer evening. Don't remember what I was doing – maybe reading or watching TV. The sun had just gone down and I glanced out the window just in time to see a great horned owl glide in from somewhere silently, silhouetted against a red sky, and land on the very top of the big spruce tree across from the house. The whole event took just a couple of seconds, and I remember feeling lucky to have witnessed it.

I might be colouring outside the lines now, but I'm thinking that much of life apart from hunting, fishing and the outdoors also involves a similar attempt to find extraordinary experiences in ordinary events, and to discover perfection amid the commonplace.

5. The Silly Side

CHARACTER(S) (2021)

So there I was, working on a bird-hunting article, explaining some of the dangerous things hunters and bird dogs can encounter out there in the woods or on the prairie. Things like snakes, skunks, porcupines, bulls, heat, cold or the farmer's dog can ruin a day pretty quickly. As I considered this I realized that our sport has some dangers as well, perhaps with more potential for exasperation than evisceration, but threats just the same.

In fly fishing, these hazards aren't animals or acts of God, you see, but instead are some of the folks we occasionally find ourselves sharing the water with, either intentionally or accidentally, and either way, regretfully. So I give you...

THE BLABBERMOUTH

He or she can't wait to tell everyone about the great fishing they've had, and where they've had it. Luckily the "platforms" available for their work are many and varied. Fly shops are great places to hold forth, as are boat ramps, fishing club meetings and of course social media. They're happy to give you the GPS co-ordinates of the hot spots as well as a short course on how to use Google Earth.

THE CURMUDGEON

This fellow occupies the opposite end of the spectrum from BM. He not only refuses to tell anyone where he fishes, he exudes something approaching contempt for those who do tell. And if his fishing is bad, he blames it not on weather, conditions or the vagaries of fish, but on other anglers and quite likely guides. "All those nutjobs on the water these days have ruined it for the rest of us!" Resist the temptation to point out that he may be one of the nutjobs in question.

THE INSTRUCTOR IN WAITING

This fellow is all enthusiasm all the time, happy to provide information to fellow anglers when requested and when not requested. He'll give you a few tips on your casting, even though he seems to have a lot of wind knots in his leader. He'll give you some tips on fly selection, even though he hasn't caught any fish yet. He's a pleasant and well-meaning sort who never lets the lack of an invitation stop him from giving some helpful advice.

"LET'S GO TOGETHER AND BUY A BOAT" GUY

It seems simple at first: "We'll partner up and split the cost three ways. Bob gets first dibs on it in May because he found the boat, I get first dibs in June, and Chuck gets first dibs in July." Sure. But Chuck discovers that the boat seems to have developed a leak while in the hands of one of the other partners. Or was it that way when Bob found the boat? The repair costs Chuck two hundred bucks, *and* the week of prime fishing that he had taken time off work to enjoy. It doesn't stop there, but you get the picture.

THE ABSENT-MINDED TINKERER

Here I simply present one of many examples: Grant and Joe were going lake fishing and asked Harold if they could borrow his tricked-out john boat. Harold said sure and thought he would help out by applying some newfangled epoxy goop to the bottom of the boat to make it slick so it would slide over rocks and gravel easily. Grant and Joe get to the lake, back the trailer into the water and begin to push the boat off the trailer. The boat doesn't move. They push harder. The boat doesn't move. The boys wonder where their strength has gone and push some more. The boat stays on the trailer. They try lifting the boat off the trailer. The boat rises a couple of inches and so does the trailer, revealing that the carpet on the deck of the trailer is firmly glued to the bottom of the boat. It seems that Harold hadn't let the fancy epoxy stuff dry long enough before putting the boat back on the trailer.

THE FLY THIEF

"I can't believe I left my fly boxes in my truck. Guess I'll have to use some of yours today. They're way better than mine anyway." Note the clever use of passive-aggressive flattery.

BUDDY WHO SAYS HE CAN ROW A DRIFT BOAT, BUT CAN'T

"Sure I can row. I do it at home in the basement all the time." This is always a very pleasant person, someone to whom you would never speak an unkind or impatient word, so he takes the oars and rows, sort of. You take the front seat and fish, sort of. In silence. With clenched teeth.

BUDDY WHO CAN ROW A DRIFT BOAT BUT SAYS HE CAN'T

Remember the last time you got an email from a "representative" of your long-lost uncle in Nigeria? This is a con job too: "Yep, ever since I tore both rotator cuffs, I can't throw a slider or row a boat at all." Funny, but he still casts pretty well.

BUDDY WHO SAYS HE CAN ROW AND CAN, BUT DOESN'T

"Wow, the day just flew by. I guess I never did take my turn at the oars. Sorry, dude."

BUDDY WHO HAS TO STOP EARLY BUT DOESN'T TELL YOU

Eventually he'll tell you, but will do so about ten minutes before he has to leave. This announcement corresponds precisely with a sudden uptick in fish activity. You get to leave then too, because you're driving. But you didn't really want to catch all those fish anyway.

TO ALL FLY FISHERS YOUNGER THAN ME (2018)

Now that I've reached the point in my life when I no longer require a fishing licence in my home province, I've started to reflect on all that being a bona fide "senior citizen" means. The first thing I've noticed is that saying it out loud takes some getting used to. It still sounds like it's coming out of somebody else's mouth. And it bugs me a little that the clerks in stores and restaurants don't seem to require proof that I'm a senior: "Oh, there's no need to see your I.D. Mr. McLennan, I believe you." And though initially I felt a little self-conscious about asking for a senior's discount on – well, anything for which a senior's discount might be available – in my brief time as a member of this club I've already learned that this feeling is easily overcome by the saving of a few bucks.

But I digress. So, young fishing partner, do you remember the time last fall when we fished my home river together? I do, specifically you and the guide working the best water for about an hour while I stumbled along the bank on my arthritic knee to find the "second best" water. And after you'd caught several good fish and lost a few more out there you hollered, "Jim, do you want to come over here and try it?" Sure, after you've completely worn out that spot? And what about the time in BC when for some unexplained reason you made a mistake and let me fish from the front seat of the boat, and I started catching more fish than you? Do you recall what happened next? I suggested trading seats, which we did immediately, and you began to catch more fish than me. And how 'bout the next day when you started out in the "good" seat and started cleaning up on fish? What did you say? You said, "We should probably trade seats at some point, huh?" And we did – about an hour later, after you'd had enough time to make sure that the hatch and the "bite" were truly over.

There's a component of this sensitive topic related to flies, as in, if you have the one that works, I need to use it or one just like it. With all the advantages your lack of first-hand experience with the golden years gives you, a little benevolent gesture now and then won't kill you. Somebody probably gave you the flies anyway. And to be reciprocal about this, if I or another old guy happens to have the effective fly, we'll be happy to loan you one similar to it as long as we've got enough for ourselves for the rest of the season.

Because fishing together as often as we do makes us almost family, and because all families have a few sensitive issues, I feel it's best to get things out in the open. So at the risk of putting forth some thoughts that could be misconstrued as self-serving, I leave you Jim's 12 Rules for Fishing with Seniors – some suggestions meant simply and genuinely to assist you and other people who occasionally have the great privilege of fishing with members of the club.

1. Seniors get the front seat of the drift boat. No feigned grace here.
2. Seniors get first shot at the best water.
3. We don't crank winch cables or change flat tires.
4. We get to pick where to stop for coffee and donuts on the way to or from the water.
5. When we need help changing flies, we get it.
6. If we think you should row the boat over to the far side of the lake, you should. Now.
7. If, or rather when, we make good casts, you should notice and say something nice, but *not*, "Hey, that's pretty good for somebody your age!"
8. If you and I catch fish that are approximately the same size, always remember that mine's bigger.
9. If you're thinking of asking me to row, remember my bad shoulder.
10. If you're thinking of asking me to drag the boat up the shore or onto the trailer, remember my bad knee.
11. If you're thinking of asking me to bring lunch, remember my bad memory.
12. Which reminds me, if I forget something at the truck, you should go back and get it.

I humbly submit these in the ongoing quest for fly-fishing harmony. Adherence to these, er, suggestions will help things go smoothly for everyone. Think of them as seniors' discounts of the piscatorial variety.

One more thing. There's a stretch of bad road on the way to the river so let's take your truck.

THE LANGUAGE OF FLY FISHING (2019)

You often hear that English is a difficult language to learn if you're not brought up with it. While that premise has merit (bearing in mind that this is coming from someone who can barely speak one language and has never seriously contemplated taking on a second), I submit that our language – the fly-fishing language – is no picnic either for a newcomer.

Neophytes are baffled by some of the terms experienced fly fishers throw around with regularity – simple terms like *upstream* and *downstream*, and others like *riffle, tailout, flat,* which aren't really difficult either, but which are probably unfamiliar if you're not in the habit of hanging out in fly shops, or reading magazines about it. And how about phrases like *drag-free drift, reach-mend, start-up inertia,* or *matching the hatch?*

These terms are sort of inherently mysterious, but there's a corner of the fly-fishing language that is founded on intentional misdirection. Leading the way here is the "Frenchman's Creek" philosophy. Frenchman's Creek is the name you use for any stream you don't want to identify. After you've used it a few times in front of the same inquisitive angler, he'll probably notice that you seem to fish Frenchman's Creek in widely differing locales. To this you can just say, "Oh, that's the north fork," or "that's lower Frenchman's." The beauty of this is that it appears initially that you're trying to be helpful, when of course you're really trying to do no such thing.

When teaching beginners about fly fishing, a lecture on the basic components of the outfit goes pretty smoothly at first. Explanations, descriptions and diagrams showing line weight and taper, rod length and reel function are met with understanding nods from the students. But when the instructor turns the page, takes a deep breath, and begins expounding (or maybe that should be "X-pounding") on the subject of leaders, things change in a hurry. Students' heads cock sideways, hands are raised, questions are asked.

The system for designating the diameter of the leader's tippet is boiled down and condensed for ease of digestion by the instructor. When he thinks he's done with this topic he somewhat reluctantly looks out and meets the students' eyes, which by now have mostly glazed over. "How 'zat again?" asks the only student brave enough to speak. The instructor circles back and tries once again to explain that the thickness of the tippet (reminding them that the tippet is the skinny end of the leader) is designated by the letter *X* with a number in front of it. This represents a measurement of the diameter of the tippet in thousandths of an inch. Hoping the student bypasses the obvious question (why don't they just use the actual measurement instead of this "x" business?) the now slightly flustered instructor explains that for every thousandth of an inch decrease in diameter, the x-designation increases by one x. So, .007 inches is 4x, .006 is 5x, .005 is 6x, and so on. He then makes a quick segue to the next topic, which is hook sizes. Here he tells the students that hook sizes are similarly identified with numbers, again with the number getting smaller as the hook gets larger. (Every time I'm the one trying to explain tippet diameter and hook size to fly-fishing students, I wonder who invented this cockamamie system where as a thing gets bigger, the number identifying its size gets smaller, and furthermore, why this person's boss would have approved such a system.)

This is just the beginning of the confusion around leaders. The poor instructor must explain that there is an important relationship between the diameter of the leader and the size of the hook the fly is tied on. "It's the rule of four," he says with feigned confidence. "Simply divide the hook size by four and that tells you what X tippet you need." Then he's expected to suggest which leader the students purchase with their first outfit, which is something they can't really do until they know the size of the first fly they're going to fish with. And of course this is information they can't possibly have, because at the moment they're in a classroom and not on a trout stream.

Another sticky spot is the term *wet fly,* which has both a general and a specific meaning. The general meaning of *wet fly* is any fly that sinks rather than floats. Yet it can also refer to a very specific type of sinking fly – the original English Wet Fly, which is constructed of soft water-absorbing materials and was the first type of fly used in the sport. Sometimes called traditional wet flies, these have fallen out of favour in recent decades, but patterns like the Iron Blue Dun, Greenwell's Glory and Partridge and Orange are still effective when fished in the original and traditional manner, cast down-and-across and swung downstream on a tight line.

So, for confusion's sake, a Wooly Bugger is a wet fly, a San Juan Worm is a wet fly, and a Partridge and Orange is a Wet Fly. A Gold-Ribbed Hare's Ear is a Wet Fly if it has wings, and is a nymph if it doesn't. In the latter case it's a wet fly, not a Wet Fly. A Light Cahill is a Wet Fly if it has down wings and soft hackle, and a dry fly if it has upright wings and stiff dry-fly hackle.

Confused? Good. Me too.

HELPFUL DEFINITIONS (2019)

WITH APOLOGIES TO ED ZERN

In an effort to continue unabated my assistance to fly fishers far and wide, I've decided it wise to clear up once and for all the unfortunate confusion created by some frequently used but misunderstood fly-fishing terms. No need to thank me.

Kamloops Trout: Mythical species of fish, conceived and promoted by the British Columbia fisheries and tourism departments in conjunction with Brian Chan, who was, not surprisingly, on the payroll for many years. See also *Loch Ness Monster*.

Pseudocloeon: A cloeon wannabe. Also called a *semi-cloeon*, not to be confused with *semi-colon,* a punctuation device used incorrectly by many fly-fishing authors.

Hot-Spotting: Recently developed manifestation of generosity, whereby with the indispensable aid of the Internet a person instantly and easily tells 18,357 other fly fishers the exact location of his favourite fishing place. Often followed by periods of deep regret, depression and harassment by former friends.

Google Earth: Extremely powerful fly-fishing tool, especially useful for facilitating hot-spotting. With its use, fly anglers are now able to reveal within a few inches' accuracy the best places to fish and which rock to stand on, using satellite photographs and GPS co-ordinates.

Frenchman's Creek: A favourite destination of deceased fly-fishing writer and novelist Robert Traver, who referred to his favourite trout stream this way because that wasn't its name. Currently declining in use as fly fishers adopt the more contemporary practice of hot-spotting. See also *north fork of the east branch of upper Frenchman's Creek.*

San Juan Worm: Best "fly" ever devised. Currently favoured by nymph fishers. Fly fishers around the world anxiously await the dry and emerger versions currently in development and undergoing rigorous testing in New Mexico.

Fluorocarbon: A controversial government tax, soon to be applied to fly fishers everywhere.

Stonefly Fishing: Obviously a typo. See Canada's new cannabis legislation.

Jack Dennis: Fictitious fly-fishing celebrity reputed to have once lived in Wyoming. Nice try. No one's ever lived in Wyoming.

Arctic Char: An often-photographed (and usually oversaturated) fish, sometimes confused with Swiss chard, which I understand may be a vegetable.

Leader Shy: A state of fear, caused by skipping work to chase a brown drake hatch, resulting in determined avoidance of employer or spouse.

Double Haul: (1) Catching twice the legal limit of fish; or (2) misspelling of *double howl,* a vocalization uttered by a person who's caught twice the legal limit of fish.

Madison River: A middling-quality trout stream, hyped by Montana's tourism department in order to deflect fly-fishing attention from other Montana streams that actually are great.

Size 24: Fictitious hook that no one has ever seen. But, hey, good joke, Tiemco, Mustad, Partridge, Daiichi et al.

Redditch Scale: Oddball sizing system, whereby the larger the thing, the smaller the number used to identify it. Inexplicably, still used today to designate hook sizes. See also *wire, thread, tippet, shot, shotguns, golf clubs,* for other nutty uses of the same principle. Devised in the Dark Ages by – you guessed it – the British.

March Brown: Another British gaffe. A mayfly that hatches in May. (It is brown, though.)

Downstream Dry Fly: A flimsy notion, presented as a factual possibility or even an intentional fly-fishing tactic (hah!), by Doug Swisher, Mike Lawson, Gary Borger, George Anderson and a myriad of other fly-fishing gurus, who obviously believe that the average fly fisher is a bit thick or at least extremely gullible. See also *Chironomid Fishing, Czech Nymphing.*

Ausable/Au Sable: The good work of several clever, forward-thinking, American fly-fishing clubs that planned and succeeded in establishing immediate inherent confusion over two different rivers in two different states, with the desired result of making bewildered fly fishers go to Maine instead.

Depuy's Spring Creek: Great fishery in Montana, the name of which is mispronounced by virtually everyone, including the family that owns it. Commonly pronounced *Dap-yooz.* Correct pronunciation, used only by Canadians, is *Du-pweez.* For other common mispronunciations of trout streams, see Popo Agie, Ahuriri, Saskatchewan and Elk (*El-ek* to people still using fill-um cameras).

Chironomid Fishing: Myth propagated by Brian Chan, Phil Rowley and other equally devious Canadian fly fishers. Sadly, the myth has been taken, hook, intermediate-line and indicator by American fly fishers.

Carp Fishing: An increasingly common spelling error, seen even in major publications. Should be *crap* fishing, as obviously no one in their right mind would fly fish for carp.

Next time: Tying a blood knot with nothing more than an electron microscope and an ordinary flux capacitor.

EXCUSES (2012)

Should we start by trying to differentiate between an excuse and a reason? Sports coaches seem to have trouble with this and can always be counted on to fiercely avoid citing a rash of team injuries as an "excuse for losing," even if it's clear to everyone else that the injuries are the reason. So if there's a difference, maybe it's that the word *excuse* carries the aroma of deception – something you try and portray as the cause of failure when it really isn't.

And fly fishing is a fertile field for creative excuses – excuses for failing to catch fish, especially when everybody else is; excuses for losing fish once they're hooked; excuses for falling in; and maybe the worst, which are excuses for not going fishing. On the latter point I've only learned one thing, but if I do say so myself it is a *universal truth*: If you wait for the perfect time to go fishing – a day when there are no jobs waiting for you at home, your calendar is completely clear, there are no important phone calls to make or receive, no meetings to attend – you'll never go. You must put a fishing day on your calendar and honour it as a commitment just like any other appointment. (And if anybody gets suspicious, just tell them you had to go to the bank.)

Once you're on the water there are a few things you can blame if the fishing doesn't pan out the way you thought it would. The weather and water conditions provide all kinds of possibilities. If the weather is too hot and bright, this is a fine excuse for not catching rainbows or browns, which everybody knows are most active on darker days. If, on the other hand, you're fishing for cutthroats, which everybody knows are the sun-worshippers of the trout family, you've got to look elsewhere for an excuse – maybe to barometric pressure, impending weather changes, or my favourite, water temperature. On a surprisingly tough day of fishing, just reach into your pack and pull out your thermometer. Hold it in the water awhile, then pick it up and look at it carefully (make sure your companion sees you doing this). Then, with a knowing smile, say something like, "Well, no wonder the fishing's tough. Look at the water temperature." This is the main reason I carry a stream thermometer.

If everything seems just right for good fishing, but you still can't buy a strike, you can turn the tables a bit with this one: conditions were probably too perfect. Sagely explain to your companions that over the years you've observed that when everything seems exactly right, the fishing is often lousy. It's as if the fish need something to stimulate their activity, like bad weather, changing barometric pressure, a full moon. "Yep, too perfect. What a shame."

You can also lean on your equipment, if necessary. I don't mean that you should simply claim that your gear is inferior (although if it is, by all means say so), but rather that you were somehow using the wrong gear: "Those fish were a long ways away, I should have been using my 6-weight rod with a weight-forward line instead of my 4-weight and that spring creek dry-fly taper." Or, "Those fish were really picky, I should have used fluorocarbon tippet and those René Harrop emergers, but I ran out of both last week on the Henry's Fork." Or my favourite, "I have a box of great hopper patterns, but I left it in the truck."

Then there's the whole business of losing fish once you've hooked them. This is a rather large category, so I'll just provide a list:

- The tip of this rod is too stiff, won't protect light tippet.
- The tip of this rod is too soft, won't set the hook properly.
- I ran out of 4x and 5x tippet and had to use 6x, which just won't handle a fish as big as that one.
- I bought these flies on the Internet and the hooks are soft and straighten out easily.
- That fish ran upstream, then turned and came straight back at me. I couldn't collect the line fast enough because I wasn't using my large-arbour reel.
- The guy at the fly shop tied my backing to my line with a faulty knot.

Something few people think about as they improve their skill and catch more and more fish is that they're systematically eliminating perfectly good excuses. But no matter how skilled you become you'll always need one from time to time, so remember this: Never ever eliminate your final excuse. What (or who) would be left to blame then?

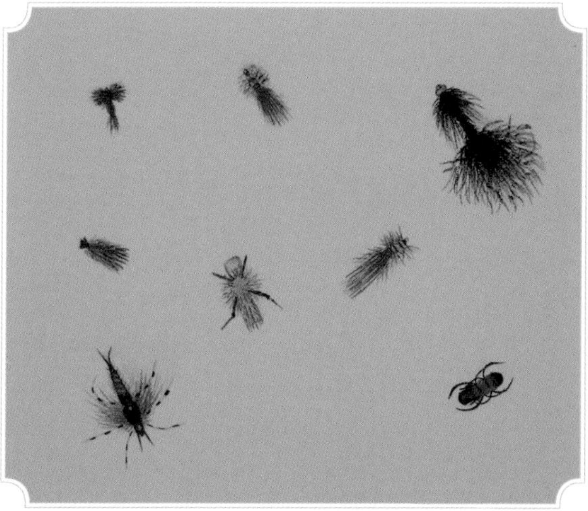

LOSING STUFF (2012)

It was one of the first float trips of summer after a long off-season. I pulled the truck over in the parking lot so I could get everything organized and into the drift boat before backing down into the boat ramp. Then, before rowing out into the river, I went through my pre-trip checklist: "Shuttle arranged, truck keys in my pocket, lunch in the cooler, cooler in the boat. That's it, we're ready to roll."

About a half-hour later I suggested that one of my companions change flies. "Let me grab a nymph from my vest for you," I said. "Now where exactly did I put my vest?" Turns out I had set it on the ground beside the boat before I backed the boat into the ramp. Now I was a mile down the river and my vest was lying on the ground back in the parking lot.

Once I realized what I had done, I stewed on it for the rest of the day, hoping I hadn't lost a fully loaded fly vest for the second time in three years. At the end of the day I drove back to the put-in spot and found the vest exactly where I had left it. It had lain in plain sight at a popular river-access spot for eight hours and no one had picked it up either to try to return it or to keep it.

These episodes rarely turn out the way this one did, but it got me thinking about how frequently I seem to lose things on fishing trips. I didn't think about it long before I realized with some relief that I'm not the only one who does it.

The propensity for losing stuff seems to comes from a number of causes, one of which is simply age – either too little or too much. With youth comes enthusiasm and exuberance, but the dark side of this is a susceptibility to distraction. When my partner and I ran a fly shop and guide service, we had a number of young guys working for us as guides. They were enthused, committed and extremely capable, but we had to watch carefully to make sure they got to the river with all the required components for their trips – things like boats, life jackets, oars, lunches and gas in the truck.

And of course middle age brings the same tendency from a more ominous direction. In the last few weeks alone my casualty list includes four spools of tippet material, one container of floatant, two cans of bear spray and two pairs of reading glasses. I can sum it up best by telling you that I haven't lost this much stuff since I was a teenager. And this list doesn't include whatever things I've lost but haven't missed yet.

It seems that the more stuff you get, the more likely you are to lose track of some of it. This is a kind of piscatorial shell game. If you have one fly rod and one reel, it's easy to keep an eye on them. But if you have, say, ten outfits and are inclined to loan, barter or sell gear from time to time, it gets more complicated. You find yourself thinking, "I'm pretty sure I had a 9-foot 4-weight rod, but I don't know if I loaned it to somebody, sold it or just can't find it."

Another factor seems to be how organized you are. If you're an "everything in its place" type of person, your stuff is probably pretty secure. However, if you're more of an "anything anyplace" type, you might have problems. This reminds me of the customer who stopped into my fly shop on his way out of town on a fishing trip: "I need some waders. I have a couple of pairs somewhere, but I can't find them, so sell me another pair, quick."

This type of behaviour leads to the occasional rediscovery of something you misplaced so long ago that you've forgotten you actually own it. It's probably an item you don't need very often, like an oddball fly line you got for a particular trip several years previous. You only used it that one time so when the opportunity for a similar trip comes around again you don't remember that you already own that line. You buy another one and then in the pre-trip packing process discover that you now have two of those oddball lines that you hardly ever use.

Some items seem to be lost more frequently than others. In this category are oars, paddles and anchors, because they're easy to miss if you're packing up in the dark after a fishing trip. Fly rods are also in this group, and the most common method of loss is setting one on the roof of the car when you return from fishing and start to pack up to go home. You nonchalantly drive away a few minutes later, having completely forgotten about the rod. A variation on this, which I've used more than once, is to lean the rod against a fence or tree and then drive away without it.

What puzzles me most about this business of losing stuff is the way it violates one of the laws of postmodern life – the one that says everything that goes around comes around. If that were true, wouldn't I be finding as much stuff as I'm losing? I'm not even close to breaking even on the deal and neither are most other fly fishers I know. So I guess it's like the odd socks you find in your drawer. Somewhere there's a big pile of stuff that fly fishers have lost over the years. Maybe we'll get it all back later at the big tackle swap in the sky.

6. At the Water

BOATS (2012)

Most people who fish, including fly fishers, have or will have some sort of experience with owning a boat. It may be a brief, passing flirtation or it may border on obsession. In either case it usually starts with the mostly logical thought that you can get to more water with a boat and therefore catch more fish. The boat might be simple, propelled only by oars, or it may be anything but simple, with big horsepower, steering wheel, windshield and an emergency backup outboard motor.

It might be a hard-sided boat made of wood, aluminum or fibreglass, or it might be made of rubber and filled with air. The most recent incarnation of the latter is the pontoon boat, and I've been fascinated to observe its evolution over the last 20 years or so. It seems to have started with what was called a float tube or belly boat that you propelled and steered by kicking your feet with the aid of swim fins. This evolved into the more user-friendly U-boat, which then morphed into today's pontoon boat, with two air chambers instead of one. Then small oars were added and after that the craft was enlarged to become a two-man pontoon boat with oars and an electric motor mount. The latest development seems to be the addition of a floor and a place for a lunch cooler. Is it just me or is this some type of circular reinvention? It seems to be pretty much the same thing we used to call an inflatable raft, which fly fishers have used for decades.

But I digress. Boats are indeed useful tools for fishing, but there are some things I feel compelled to advise you about, starting with this: "A boat is a hole in the water into which one pours money." Nobody seems to know who came up with that line, but it's a great one that's also true. Once you own a boat there are always upkeep costs and more accessory gizmos you can get that *might* help you catch more fish, but *will* cost you more money.

I've only owned three boats. The first was a 12-foot aluminum car-topper that I stole from and then inherited from my father. He and I used this to fish the trout lakes of Jasper National Park when I was growing up, and I later used it on moving water, where it proved to be a little lacking in, shall we say, river-worthiness. I hoodwinked a friend into buying it from me, and the last time I saw it, it was in his garage, filled with showshoes, some elk antlers and a portable duck blind.

Next came an aluminum john boat, which was the most versatile of my modest fleet. Its olive drab colour and flat bottom made it a good platform from which to shoot ducks, and it would also take an outboard motor. What I used it for mainly, though, was float-fishing a large, gentle trout river, where it performed admirably. But as fly fishing boomed in the '90s, john boats went out of fashion and almost everybody else on the river started rowing what were then called McKenzie River drift boats. I didn't want to be the last guy to the party, so of course I had to get one of those. I sold the john boat to another unsuspecting friend and bought a nice, used, wooden drift boat. This was probably my favourite boat, because it rowed well, looked great and made me feel that I was a sophisticated fly fisher who was up with the times and also had an obvious appreciation for tradition. I didn't mind, either, that other fishermen always seemed to admire the pretty wooden boat.

But because it was made of wood, this boat needed maintenance every couple of years. Since I am a mechanically challenged individual, this meant that I needed other people to do the work. So at least four and possibly five times, I found friends who had the knowledge, interest, tools, garage space and, most importantly, the gullibility to take on the tasks of refinishing, repairing, repainting and whatever else the boat needed. It is worth noting, I suppose, that no one individual worked on it twice. All had found it to be more work and less fun than they expected.

After about 15 years I realized I was running out of the right kind of friends, and concluded that people like me should never own any piece of equipment that requires frequent maintenance. So I sold the boat a year or so ago to another fishing buddy, who immediately refinished and refurbished it. The boat looks great again, he loves it, and I'm satisfied that it is he who should own it.

I now borrow a boat when I need one. The main problem with this is in figuring out how to operate all the clever but complicated and puzzling systems for anchors, oarlocks, hitches, straps and covers, and then putting them all back together properly before I return the boat.

So that's my life with boats so far. Along the way I've learned other important lessons – too many of them the hard way – about the importance of details like drain plugs, spare oars, anchors, life jackets and tool kits.

I've also found some other people with experience similar to mine and we're considering starting an organization called Recovering Boaters Anonymous. Send me an email if you think you need help. No need to include your name.

AT HOME ON THE BOW (2013)

Few people love rivers as fly fishers do. That's partly because fly fishing produces a deep connection between the participant and the location, and partly because the rivers where fly fishing happens are easy places to love. What's more, the sport of fly fishing asks you – no – *requires* you – to learn about the fish, their habitat, their food and how they go about their day-to-day business. Over time this learning begets an appreciation for the river and its occupants. Appreciation grows into something else – a kind of intimacy, perhaps, and then affection – a profound affection for the unique blend of sights, sounds, aromas and events that define a day on a trout stream.

And while fly fishers love all their rivers, most have one that receives more of their affection and attention than the rest. This one is the fly fisher's "home water."

For more than 40 years my home water has been the Bow River – Alberta's mountain stream turned prairie river that bisects the city of Calgary. I met the Bow as many do – through the introduction of a friend. I was a teenager in the early stages of what was to become a lifelong and unexplainable obsession with the quiet art of fly fishing. It was October 1970, the days of the FLQ crisis in Canada, and after 20 minutes and a dozen casts into the Bow both the young fly fisher and a couple of trout were hooked. At its most elemental level, what got me that day was the size and strength of the trout – bigger and stronger than any I had caught anywhere before.

Ours was a long-distance relationship until 1975, when I started guiding fly fishers on the river. The guiding business was slow initially, but that didn't bother me, as I was happy for the frequent "days off" from guiding that became exploratory days when I fished alone or with friends, soaking up what the river and the fish could teach me. Of course I easily rationalized this as "research" that would help me be a better guide when more customers arrived.

And arrive they did, after some high-profile American outdoor writers sampled the river in the late '70s and early '80s and wrote glowing reports in US outdoor magazines. In typical Canadian fashion, it took the validation of experts from "the south" to convince us we had something special in our own neighbourhood. As a result of the good press, the Bow became famous in fly-fishing circles through the '80s and '90s. Guide services, fly-fishing stores and other related businesses appeared in Calgary, and are still there, running guide trips, selling flies and tackle, and dispensing knowledge and advice to local fly fishers and visitors from around the globe.

In my time with the Bow and its rainbow and brown trout, I've had much great fishing, but in the early days I was uneasy with apprehension as the oil-crazy Cowtown pumpjacked its way to prosperity with little concern for much else. Through Calgary's growth from 385,000 inhabitants in 1970 to 1.1 million in 2013, the river faced and withstood numerous water-quality issues, and sidestepped the dire possibilities that come simply from existing so close to so many humans.

In the 1980s, Trout Unlimited Canada arrived in Calgary with its mandate to conserve, protect and restore freshwater ecosystems. Its presence has helped raise the river's profile both with sportsmen and with the city and province. The Bow has more friends and protectors today than ever before, and both civic and provincial governments have slowly come to realize the economic value of a trout stream like the Bow, and have given its health greater priority than it once had.

It's a lamentable truth that something as crass as "economic value" must be the incentive to protect something as magnificent as a trout stream. Shouldn't aesthetic beauty, historical significance and ecological uniqueness be enough? Should be, but, sadly, are not.

The Bow downstream of the city is indeed a beautiful place. A mix of high, timbered banks, low gravel flats, islands and side channels, it's home to whitetail and mule deer, the occasional moose, and beavers, white pelicans, osprey and eagles. Shore birds putter about on the gravel, a "V" of Canada geese tilts against thunderheads gathering in the west, all a perfect backdrop for the fly fisher who wades the shallows carefully, looking for feeding trout.

The Bow is a memory maker, and its many admirers all have their favourites. Perhaps most significant to me is the way this big, gentle river has been embraced by my family. The first to share my infatuation with the Bow was my wife Lynda, then our daughter Deanna, who literally grew up on the river, and more recently, son-in-law Brandon, who learned his way around the Bow under the tutelage of Deanna. It pleases me greatly to know that these two will continue to add to their own album of Bow River memories long after mine is closed.

I've seen three severe floods on the Bow, in 1995, 2005 and the most severe in June 2013. On each previous occasion I and others worried about the river's future as a trout stream (after first worrying about the effects of the flood on people and property). What happens to the fish when the river grows in volume 30-fold in a matter of hours? What happens to the aquatic insects, the trout's most important food? Are they pulverized into bug powder? An inquiry to an expert, Oregon aquatic entomologist and fly fisher Rick Hafele, brings some comfort: "The short answer is that aquatic insects and trout have evolved to deal with floods. Insects move down into the substrate to over a meter deep. Many young insect nymphs and larvae spend most of their time in this 'hyporheic zone,' thus when floods occur they are not affected much. In many ways aquatic insects are better adapted to floods than humans."

The trout themselves generally respond to floods by moving to the edges of the river where friction reduces current velocity. The problem is that in a flood many of these "edges" are some distance from the river channel. As the water recedes, the fish follow it back to the river channel, but some fish are stranded in isolated pieces of water. The extent of the problem in 2013 wasn't known until the water receded, and a number of individuals and organizations then undertook "fish rescues" to find stranded fish and return them to the river.

The previous floods in my lifetime demonstrated the unusual strength and resiliency of rivers, for the Bow returned to its glory sooner than nearly everyone expected. And though it will take some time before it returns to what we have come to think of as "normal" after this flood, when the water recedes and clears I'm quite certain I'll find myself there, casting on the waters of the great and once-again gentle Bow. And as I have for 44 seasons, I'll hope my fly is found by one of the extraordinary trout that live in this extraordinary river.

2013 (2014)

Reflecting on the "Great Flood of 2013" in southern Alberta, which was the worst in the province's history, I was reminded of one of the great truths of fishing – fishing of any type. That truth is simply this: Change Rules All.

We want our streams, rivers and lakes to stay the same, but they won't, they can't and they shouldn't. The only thing that's sure about next season is that it won't be just like this one. It will be better, worse, different. Aside from our angler's annoyance with this fact, it sometimes gets a bit dicey because the assumption that noticeable changes are part of natural cycling can sometimes disguise a problem with a fishery. If the fishing drops off over a couple of years, is it a natural function of the variability that is inherent in rivers and lakes, or is there really something wrong out there? For example, it seems I'm finding fewer mountain whitefish in the streams I fish. Is this a natural fluctuation in their population, or is something going on that we should investigate more carefully?

The fishing in Alberta in the summer of 2013 was unlike any I remember. Every trip to a familiar place was like a first visit to a new place. River channels had moved, corners were straightened, some islands appeared, others disappeared, and deadfall lined the banks and littered the forest next to the streams.

As fishers we spend a lot of time learning what makes our favourite fisheries tick. Just when we feel we've gotten to know what's going on, something (or, as in Alberta in 2013, *everything*) changes, and we don't like it. Maybe it's our arrogant and deep-seated human sense of entitlement that causes us to be offended. We want our favourite places to always be the way we remember them, but they won't be, at least not for long. The rock that marked the perfect casting spot might be gone one day. That beautiful deep pool may become a shallow, swift riffle. What are we supposed to do then? Start over? Yes.

The fishing people I feel most sympathy for are professional guides who are paid for their intimate and current knowledge of their water. But when sudden change comes, they're in the same boat (so to speak) as everyone else, trying to read the "new" water, think about the implications of the changes, and still get their clients in to fish. The guides who already consider their streams and lakes to be moving targets and who expect to have to adapt are best at this. Those who head for the same spots and fish them the same way they always have will not do as well.

Last summer I fished a familiar stream after it finally cleared and dropped to a nice level. I parked at one of my usual access spots and walked through the woods to the edge of the river.

"Hmm," I thought as I surveyed a brand new stream. "Didn't the river used to be over there?" I wondered, looking at a somewhat familiar stand of trees a couple of hundred yards away across the rubble of rocks, boulders and deadfall. Nonetheless, the water in front of me was inviting, so I stepped in. My companion and I fished for an hour or two with no good results. I stewed about this and eventually came upon the thought that we were fishing in a place that was forest last season. Granted, the bottom looked normal for this stream – a mix of rocks and small boulders. The pool we were in looked good too – a fallen tree at the bank and a deep, turquoise run of medium-speed water right next to it. We saw no fish rise and caught no trout. I continued thinking. So if these rocks were underneath the forest last season, and they've been suddenly transformed into a stream bottom, how much aquatic life is there down in those rocks and boulders now? I didn't excavate to find out, but I doubt there was very much, except for those buggy individuals that moved in with the water when the river changed course. But I've been told by aquatic entomologists that many of the aquatic insects that trout eat burrow down into the substrate to find safety in times of flood. So where I was fishing there was a river but no aquatic bugs, while over there where the river used to be, mightn't there be (or mightn't there have been for a time) some aquatic bugs but no river? This, of course, is the convoluted speculation of a layman, and I've consulted no scientists about it.

The critters that live in places like this – trout, aquatic insects, muskrats, beavers, herons, kingfishers, ospreys and others – adapt. They've been adapting for centuries. It's us that have trouble with it, and we're supposed to be the smart ones.

How did that great pool you love so much on your favourite stream get to be like that? Answer: By changing from what it was before.

So here's my dilemma: Should I stop now, or carry on and take the low-hanging fruit by expanding this fishing topic into a life lesson? How about I just say that the inevitability of change – in any part of life – is something we need to get a better handle on.

WATER MUSIC (2015)

Few things catch and hold my attention the way fire and water do. Anybody who's ever sat around a campfire will agree that when you're near it your eyes are drawn to the constantly changing flames. And since you're reading this story, I'm guessing that, like mine, your eyes are drawn to the moving water of a river or stream in much the same way.

So why does the sight of water – especially moving water – fascinate us so? For starters, people who like to fish have developed the habit of staring at the water to try and figure out where the fish are likely to be. Some of us have it so bad that it's simply impossible to avoid looking at the water. You know you're in this group if you find yourself glancing down at your favourite stream, or indeed any piece of moving water whenever you cross one in your vehicle. You might think, "I've never fished this section before. It looks pretty good, nice and clear, the level looks fine. There's a great-looking gravel bar over on the far side. Wait – was that a rise?" Distracted driving, anyone?

The sound of moving water is another topic, one with more variations in its appeal. The music of moving water is played by an ensemble of many instruments. There's the high-range, glassy clatter of a small stream flowing swiftly over gravel. There are the percussive low thumps of a big river pounding into big boulders. There's the friendly, crystalline hum of a delicate spring creek, its sounds fairly insisting that there must be trout rising.

The sound of moving water stimulates thought – often of a quietly meditative, reflective nature. Perhaps it's the rhythm and cadence of moving water that does it. Human music promotes the same kind of thought. So is it a stretch to suggest that this might be one of the reasons so many skilled musicians are anglers, especially fly fishers? The list is long and includes people like Eric Clapton, Huey Lewis, Adrian Smith, Christopher Parkening and a host of less famous "fishin' musicians."

Ever notice how the sound of even a small creek increases in volume as the sun goes down? I can't explain why this happens, but I know it helps people sleep at night. My favourite example occurs at a friend's cabin in the foothills. The cabin sits at the edge of a high bluff above a good trout stream. In the daytime, when we're wandering around the cabin, sorting tackle, making a meal or just telling lies on the deck, we don't hear the creek. But when it's dark and I'm lying in the loft with the window open, the river's sounds are very audible, and it's the main reason I sleep better there than almost anywhere else.

One day years ago I fished my way up a small brown trout stream. Nothing was happening so I sat down on the bank and ate a sandwich, and then, in what's becoming a common component of my fishing trips, I made a rough pillow out of my fishing vest and lay down on the bank with my head on the vest and my feet in the water. Then the water did its thing, making sounds that were gentle, soothing and sleep-inducing. I nodded off and dozed for an undetermined length of time until the sound of the creek changed very slightly. Its rhythmic chuckle was interrupted by a quiet, gentle *thuk* every few seconds. As subtle as this sound was, it burrowed into my subconscious mind because it was new. I don't know how long it took, but eventually, through the fog of my sleep, I realized that along with the sound of water moving over the gravel, I was hearing the sound of a trout feeding on the surface. I sat up, rubbed my eyes, looked over and found the source of the *thuk* just a few metres from where I had been napping. I checked my fly, made a cast without getting up, yawned and caught the fish.

I believe that the sounds, as well as the sights and aromas, of the places we fish become significant parts of the memories we make on the water. Our conscious memory takes care of the obvious stuff – it was a cloudy day, the fishing was great, I caught a 23-inch brown on a Pale Morning Dun. But our subconscious mind grabs and holds the subtler components of a memory – the sound of the water on that stream at that spot on that day, the smell of the blooming wolf willow along the banks, the sight of dainty mayflies dancing against the setting sun. These form the fundamental essence of a memory, and when we encounter one of these stimuli in an unexpected context, our minds are immediately drawn back to a specific event in which this sight, sound or aroma was part of the backdrop. I'm no psychologist, but this might make a case that the subconscious mind is stronger than the conscious.

Still water plays a different kind of music, for many of the sounds come from goings-on around the water rather than the water itself. One of the most "alive" of all ecosystems is a marshy prairie lake, the kind of place where northern pike live. Visit one of these places in the spring and you'll probably be surprised by the distinct lack of quietude. The prairie lake's musicians are primarily birds, frogs, insects, occasionally fish, and the nearly constant prairie breeze that bows the strings of the willow and poplar trees. There's very little silence around such a place. And I'm sure we've all noticed how still water amplifies sounds around it, particularly in the evening. You can clearly hear conversations from a quarter mile away over still water on a calm evening.

Why do people like to live near water? Of course there's the obvious pragmatic reason – that water is required for life and if water is handy, life is simpler. But other more aesthetically based attractions are reasons also. Aside from the fact that people need water, they also simply like to live within sight of it, and dare I say, within hearing range of the water's music. The real estate profession has confirmed this, as property that's bounded by water is always more expensive that property that's not.

The music made by water means different things to different people. In the study of art this might be called "freedom of interpretation." Anglers hear the gentle clatter of moving water as an invitation to participate in their chosen sport. Canoeists and kayakers hear the roar of Class IV rapids as a call to a thrilling ride. Farmers might hear running water in the spring as a kind of promise and the hope for a bumper crop that could pay for a nice holiday next winter. Engineers and dam builders might hear something different.

Perhaps moving water, with its paradoxical qualities of fluidity and shape, sound and silence, somehow reflects the path of a human life. Moving water is always coming, always going; never the same today as it was yesterday or will be tomorrow.

7. People

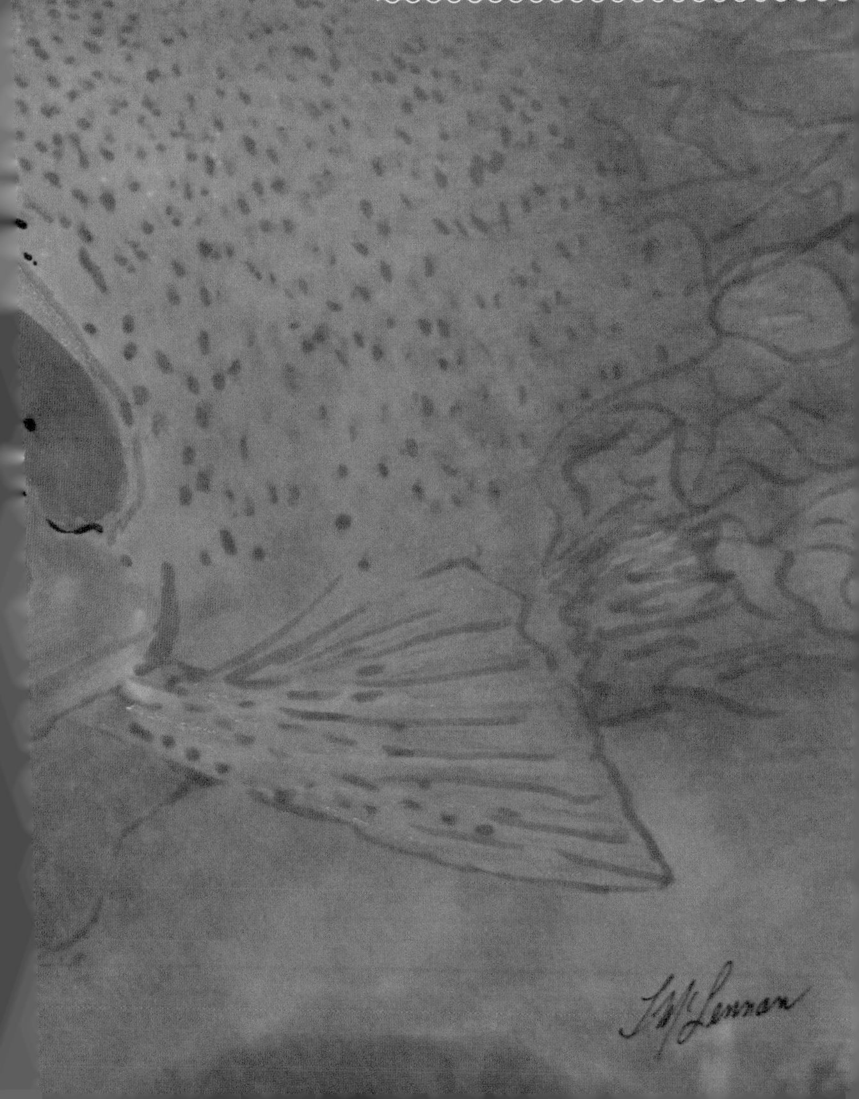

MENTORS (2012)

The dictionary definition of *mentor* is "an experienced and trusted advisor," and although the term has become quite trendy, that doesn't change the fact that it is good and useful as both a word and an idea.

In the fly-fishing world, mentors come in many forms. They are often fathers, uncles or family friends, but can also be someone you meet on the water, at a fishing club or in a fly shop. A mentor can be almost anyone who has more fly-fishing experience than you do, as long as he also has the right attitude. As Lefty Kreh has pointed out, there's a huge difference between sharing knowledge and simply displaying knowledge.

I suppose part of mentorship is the idea of a well-experienced veteran helping a less-experienced angler improve his skills. In this regard I've been more fortunate than anyone I know, simply because of circumstances in my earlier fly-fishing years. When I was in my mid-20s I was the only full-time guide on a river that was just beginning to gain an international reputation. All the big-time fly-fishing writers of the day wanted to fish this river, and from the mid-'70s to the early '80s, when the big guys came, they usually ended up fishing with me. I've certainly frittered away some opportunities in my life, but during these years I was smart enough to take advantage of the situation every time it came along. As a result I learned directly from men like Lefty Kreh, Ernest Schwiebert, A.J. McClane, Gary Borger, Charley Waterman and Charles Brooks, all of whom were on my list of fly-fishing heroes. I asked them questions, I watched them fish, I asked more questions. I examined their tackle, watched them fish some more, asked more questions. In the non-fly-fishing world, it was the equivalent of a green kid carrying clubs for Palmer, Nicklaus and Snead.

I saw these people infrequently, though, so while I learned much from them, I couldn't call them true mentors. A true mentor is someone with whom you have an ongoing relationship, and someone who is a kind of "spiritual director" rather than just a passer-on of skill. A mentor is a person who draws you into an understanding of and appreciation for the peripheral, yet still crucial, parts of the endeavour.

In that regard I've also been extremely fortunate. The man who stands out more than the others is a friend of my father's – a man I met when I was 8 years old. He was an experienced outdoorsman then and he's someone I maintain a relationship with to this day. One of my earliest memories is of him taking me out on the lawn in front of my parents' house and showing me how to double haul, when I was about 12. Later, during our occasional times together fishing and hunting, I learned more from him by watching and asking questions. Later still, when I was ready to understand, he made me realize that the experience is never just about the fishing or the shooting. There's always more to it than that, and these other elements are the things you can rely on, savour and recall fondly. He taught me to both expect and enjoy the partial successes and near misses that in truth characterize most of our outdoor adventures. Now that he's getting on and I'm at least middle-aged, this is what I remember learning from him, more than the things he showed me about casting and fishing technique.

There is a marvelous book that illustrates mentorship in a most poignant way. The book is *The Earth Is Enough,* by Harry Middleton, and in it the main character, a young man traumatized by events in Vietnam, goes to live with his grandfather and uncle who are subsistence farmers in the Ozark Mountains. The men are also naturalists, hunters, fly fishers, philosophers and fans of the blues, and as they teach the young man about these things they teach him about life. They are mentors in the truest sense of the word, for they not only show him the practical, necessary skills – that is, the *hows* of such a life, but they pull back the curtain on far more important things: the need to have respect for the land and the water and the way wild creatures live and die, and the fact that integrity must always guide our intercourse with the land and the water. These are the *whys,* the principles that define and reveal the soul of an outdoor life.

So here's to true mentors, the people who show us where the fish hide in the stream, what fly to fool them with, and then, when the day is over, help us understand that in fly fishing, as in the rest of life, the journey is far more important than the destination.

ARTISTS (2017)

In the last few years my wife Lynda has taken up drawing and painting – things she had not attempted before. As it turns out she seems to have a knack for it and has presented members of our family with sketches and paintings of various subjects, including, as you might expect, rivers, fish, bird dogs and grandchildren.

This surprising turn in our own house has made me think more about art in general, which is far too big a topic for this space. But art as it relates to fly fishing is a smaller topic and one I'm willing to blather about regardless of my lack of qualification.

Though it is an art of equal stature, I'm not thinking of photography. Painting and drawing are different from photography the way fiction writing is different from non-fiction. A fiction writer is not completely bound by reality, although I've known experienced fiction writers who have told me they are, and must be, firmly bound by their character's personalities, to the point where the characters eventually "drive the bus" in creating the story.

It seems that if you're drawing or painting, you're likewise not bound tightly to reality. In fact, for some artists the job may be to intentionally bend reality a little, so that it remains recognizable but perhaps says something different to a viewer than just what's apparent at the surface.

Our daughter is a choreographer, and when I see one of her dance works performed, afterward she usually asks, "What did the piece mean to you?" I'm a little fumbly with my response, but if I reply with "What's it supposed to mean?" she usually says, "I know what it means to me, but it's not necessary for it to mean the same thing to you. What's important is that it says *something* to you." It seems that this breadth of interpretation is one of the things that makes dance, painting, and indeed all art, unique and compelling.

Artists, photographers, and possibly writers approach most things, including and especially fly fishing, a little differently than other folks. They can't help but see the possibilities that our stimulating and beauty-intense sport places before them. And artists have the great ability to notice the small details of the drama. If Lynda and I are fishing, I might be looking upriver, simultaneously trying to see if there are any bugs in the air or rising fish in the water while also scanning the horizon to see what the weather might do. Lynda lags behind because she's found a stonefly nymph that's just crawled out of the water and is emerging into adulthood on a rock. Her camera comes out to record the event because she might want to paint it someday.

Later, if I catch a fish, I'll proudly show it to her, and of course she wants to take a photograph, but not the kind I'm thinking of. For instance, she might want a shot of the fish's adipose fin. Just the adipose fin. "Look at the shape and colours there," she'll say excitedly. "I've never noticed that balance and symmetry before." "Uh, okay," I say, trying to quell my desire to get back to the fish-catching part of the outing.

I've never understood how these kinds of artists do what they do, and I'm pretty sure it's a gift – one that I don't have. And that's why I have huge admiration for all artists, especially those who bring it home to me by creating inspiring images of the things I love to do, the creatures I do them with, and the places I do it. Artists like Diane Michelin, Derek DeYoung, Karl Geist and Allan Hassall, along with those of an earlier generation like Jack Cowin, Eldridge Hardie, Russell Chatham, Chet Reneson and many more I'm leaving out but shouldn't, are magicians. I see what they've done, I'm immediately moved by it, and I have no clue how they did it.

Can art and artists teach us something about fly fishing? I think they can. They might not help us catch more fish, but there are already plenty of ways to learn that. The purpose of fly-fishing art, like the purpose of all art, I surmise, is to move us, make us feel something, cause us to think. The best angling art brings to me an emotional response similar to the one I experience when I'm in the act of fishing. Sometimes an artist's rendering of a rather common element – a fish or a fly pattern perhaps – makes me see something I didn't know was really there. When I look at a painting of a brown trout, for instance, I might see colours that I hadn't noticed on the real fish. So the next time I inspect a brown trout I've caught, I look for those colours and, sure enough, there they are, released from hiding. It's something I wouldn't have seen if not for the clear, perceptive eyes of an artist.

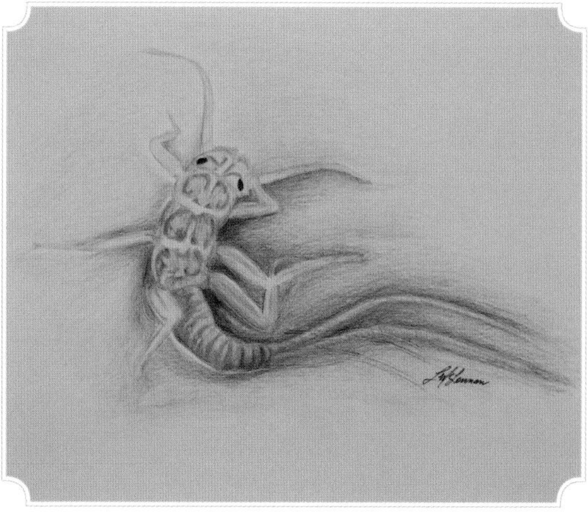

GRANDPARENTING (2020)

In the most unusual COVID times in 2020 it was perhaps understandable that someone my age – or any age, I suppose – should begin to think about what's around the corner. That's the big corner: the future. So, coronavirus notwithstanding, I'm aware that with two grandsons soon to reach the age of maturity – which of course in these circles means the age when they're able to cast fly lines – Lynda and I find ourselves pondering the degree to which these little guys will be drawn to this activity that's been so central to our family's life. We're trying to temper our hope with enough wisdom to avoid pushing too hard toward this goal because that might have the opposite effect.

Of course we think we've got this covered so far, as at ages 6 and 4, they've already been introduced to fish, fishing, trout-bugs and most of the other related stuff we obsess over. And while there seems to be some genuine interest there, we're trying to remember how we approached this with the boys' mother, because whatever we did with her clearly worked. We were reminded of this last summer when we watched this young mother kneeling at the water's edge with a trout she'd caught, two small blonde heads leaning over and looking in, two sets of tiny hands reaching to touch tentatively. With luck and wise counsel from the boys' elders it's our hope that this fascination will continue and they'll come to be at least as interested in the natural world as the digital world.

But I also wonder if we fly-fishing parents and grandparents are aiming high enough. Are we using fly fishing to teach our offspring something more important than fly fishing itself? I think we're all pretty much aware of the fact that playing in the water the way we do can lead (should lead? must lead?) to caring for the things that live in the water, and that caring for the things that live in the water must lead to caring for the water itself as well as the other things that depend on the water.

The sport itself will probably take care of some of this. History is full of examples of how participation in the "field sports" of hunting and fishing has led people into significant roles in conservation. To paraphrase one of my fly-fishing mentors, "If you're going to use a resource for recreation, you have an obligation to protect and preserve the resource that provides that recreation." Indeed, it's hard to find a major conservation leader who hasn't come to that belief and commitment through the portal of hunting or fishing. Research the founders of organizations like Ducks Unlimited, Trout Unlimited, Atlantic Salmon Federation, Bonefish & Tarpon Trust, Steelhead Society and other groups to confirm this.

So our boys' parents and grandparents will keep talking, teaching and taking the little guys fishing, hunting, bug catching and anything else that it seems might interest them in the outdoors (except possibly ice fishing – but I digress). One day before long we'll show up at their house with an indoor yarn-rod and watch them cast at each other, possibly knocking stuff off the bookshelves and breaking the odd thing, but while they're at it hopefully also beginning to get the feel of casting. And in time we'll ask (gently, of course) if they want to try tying flies, which might mean we'll have to turn part of their house or ours into a "tying room."

We'll continue our low-key but important outings to the water, which we'll call "fishing trips," but which will be centred around having fun doing whatever the little guys find interesting, whether it involves trying to catch fish or not. Rock throwing, bug catching, and frog watching can all be important parts of a fishing trip. And if we're true to our purpose and goal, while we're enjoying these times we'll also talk with them about water and the larger purposes it serves.

Of course Lynda and I look forward to the days when they cast to and catch the first fish of their own, and a little later to the time when we have to holler at them with feigned annoyance as darkness approaches, "Come on you two! It's late. We've got to stop now. No more 'last casts.'" Those days will be significant marking points, but they're not the end of the story, are they?

I've made the statement before that one of fly fishing's greatest benefits to its practitioners is the simple fact that it isn't nearly as important as many other things in life. But that doesn't let us off the hook. I think we must be intentional in directing new fly fishers of all ages toward the goal of conserving the water and the things that live in it and depend on it. I'm quite certain we all want to keep playing in the water.

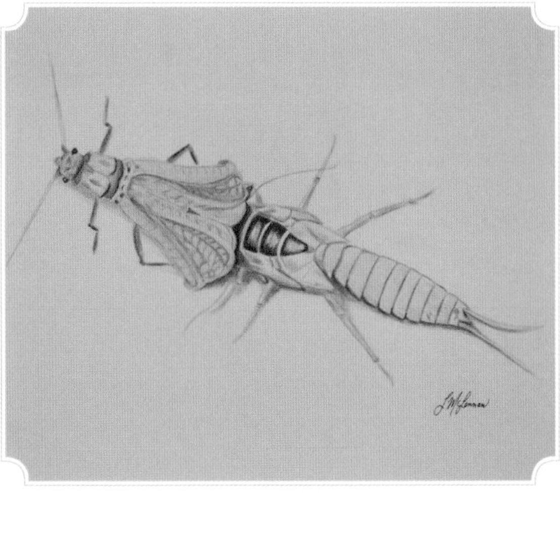

THE INFLUENCERS (2012)

Like all activities that grow and evolve over time, fly fishing has derived huge benefit from those who came before – the ones we could call trailblazers. These people fished with simpler tackle, with less technical innovation and without the benefit of easy travel to exotic destinations. Yet they took the sport to new places, literally and figuratively. They fished for new species, invented new tackle and flies, came up with new ideas and new understandings of fish and the creatures they eat. In short, they expanded the sport, forcing it to become something more than a quirky hobby brought over from the old country by a few eccentrics dressed in tweed. They taught us how to think about fly fishing and made us understand that it has an important role to play in the conservation of wild things and wild places.

The common ground, the point of contact between these people and us, is easy to identify. It is passion for the sport. Somewhere along the road, for them and for us, we became enthralled by the possibility, remote as it might be at times, of a fish taking a fly that we have cast.

It wasn't so much that fly fishing's groundbreakers decided to be innovators or explorers or philosophers; driven by the passion, they simply couldn't help themselves.

So who were some of the most important "influencers" of fly fishing through the last 50 years? Here, in no particular order, is one observer's list.

LEFTY KREH

In fly-fishing conversations, when the name "Lefty" is mentioned, nobody ever asks, "Lefty who?" For like "Michael" in basketball and "Wayne" in hockey, a first name is all that's required.

Lefty, whose real first name was Bernard, and who was not left-handed but ambidextrous, was one of those guys who was good at everything he did. Known in our circles for his fly-fishing expertise, he was also a bait and plug-fishing expert and in his younger days an exhibition trick shooter. Lefty probably fished for more species of fish with fly tackle than anybody and was one of the early developers of methods, tackle and flies for tropical saltwater fly fishing, along the way creating arguably the best saltwater fly ever – the Lefty's Deceiver. But his most enduring contribution to our sport might be the way he pushed us all to become better fly casters. An ambidextrous casting phenom himself, he did more than anyone to turn the average duffer into a more effective and efficient fly caster. He was also an active outdoor writer for well more than half a century, and wrote or co-authored more than 30 books. Lefty was the face of our sport until and beyond his death in 2018 at age 93.

GARY LAFONTAINE

Gary died in 2002 of Lou Gehrig's Disease, and with his death, fly fishing suffered. Perhaps the most original thinker of the modern era in this field, he was never satisfied with what was thought to be true about trout and fooling them with flies. His books, including *Caddisflies*, *The Dry Fly: New Angles*, and *Trout Flies: Proven Patterns*, delve into and explore concepts rarely considered before, such as the effect of the type of light (midday versus late evening) on the trout's perception of our imitations, and the "triggering factors" that convince a trout to accept our imitation. Many of LaFontaine's original patterns look strange to the human eye and could be summarily tossed into the Oddball File, except for one thing: they were designed after extensive consideration of the trout's physiology and behaviour, after numerous prototype assessments, and after underwater observation of both the fish and the food item the fly is supposed to imitate. Gary could tell you (and did, in his books and speaking engagements) why his Mohawk and Mess patterns look the way they do, and why and when they work. He had a deep-rooted aversion to the idea that "we do it that way because that's the way we do it." Gary was an original and we miss his way of thinking.

JOE BROOKS

Fly-fishing travel may have begun in earnest with Joe Brooks. Strongly associated with the early days of fly fishing in the Florida Keys, Joe and his wife Mary were pioneers of fly fishing in South America, Africa and the south Pacific. Brooks also was largely responsible for "discovering" the great fly fishing for trout in the Rocky Mountain West and for introducing Lefty to the sport. Brooks's magazine stories about his trips to Montana, particularly the Yellowstone River, where he fished big streamers for outrageous brown trout, caught the attention of fly fishers and began to draw them to Montana and other western states so they could experience what he wrote about. Brooks was "inclusive" in his approach, and his message was that fly fishing is easy and anybody can do it.

GARY BORGER

An educator by profession, Wisconsin's Gary Borger is perhaps fly fishing's best pure teacher. Known mainly as a trout guy, he embraced what was in the 1980s a new concept, namely filming fly fishing events and turning them into educational videos that fly fishers could watch and learn from at home.

Borger's numerous books support and amplify the information presented in his videos. Titles like *Nymphing, Naturals* and *Designing Trout Flies* provide us with a vast volume of information to take to our own waters. Perhaps his most valuable lesson for us lies in his fresh way of thinking. Gary regularly strips away the unnecessary things we might have thought essential to fly fishing, and leaves us a simpler way of accomplishing the goal.

LEE WULFF

Perhaps more responsible than anyone else for the development and publicizing of fly fishing in the 20th century, Wulff is likely the only true legendary figure in our sport. Among his many "credits" are the invention of the fly-fishing vest, the creation of the Wulff series of dry flies, the pursuit and capture of huge Atlantic salmon on tiny fly rods, and the concept of catch-and-release fishing, articulated in his famous 1936 statement that "game fish are too valuable to only be caught once." With his wife Joan, he developed one of North America's first fly-fishing schools on the Beaverkill River in New York state.

Wulff brought many of his fishing adventures – especially with Atlantic salmon – to life by filming them. These films are still around and are still impressive. Along the way he wrote eight books, including *Leaping Silver*, an homage to the Atlantic salmon. In the 1940s Wulff established a fishing camp in Newfoundland, from which he explored salmon rivers with his float plane. One of fly fishing's greatest ambassadors, he died at 86, in a plane crash while renewing his pilot's licence.

ERNEST SCHWIEBERT

Unlike TV sitcoms, which seem obligated to portray all fishermen as bumbling oafs, the late Ernest G. Schwiebert Jr. believed that fly fishers should be the intellectuals of the outdoors. An architect by profession, he was one of the first North American fly fishers, along with Art Flick, to become infatuated with the aquatic insects trout feed on. Whereas Flick acquired intimate knowledge of the insect life on his home stream in the Catskills of New York state, Schwiebert, being an erudite, world-travelling angler, applied fly-fishing entomology more broadly. His 1955 book, *Matching the Hatch*, written while he was a student at Ohio State University, was one of fly fishing's first "bug books." It stressed the importance to fly fishers of understanding the life cycles, habitat, behaviour and emergence activity of the aquatic insects trout eat. His 1978 book, *Trout*, is 1,700 pages of scholarly, passionate, fly-fishing knowledge, for which he also did the illustrations.

Schwiebert convinced many of us that it's better to know something about what we are imitating, and convinced us that fishing this way brings both more success and more satisfaction. Other prominent fly-fishing writers followed his lead, including Doug Swisher and Carl Richards, Rick Hafele, Dave Hughes, Dave Whitlock and others. Some of the things fly fishers now consider common knowledge became that because of the work of Schwiebert and those he inspired. After Schwiebert, it was no longer good enough to throw a "little brown fly" out there to imitate those "little brown bugs."

RODERICK HAIG-BROWN

An ex-pat Brit who moved to Canada's Vancouver Island and became a provincial magistrate and chancellor of the University of Victoria, Haig-Brown pointed us toward the beauty of our sport and found words most others can't for explaining why we love it so. A writer who fly fished, rather than a fly fisher who wrote, he showed us the literary side of our sport. He also taught us to study the fish and their environments, both so we could catch more fish and so we would appreciate them aside from simply trying to catch them. He is often regarded as the best pure writer fly fishing has produced, and perhaps the strongest testimonial to Haig-Brown's exceptional writing skill is the frequency with which his words are chosen to represent the aesthetics of fly fishing. You'll find lines from his book *A River Never Sleeps* quoted frequently, like these: "A river is never quite silent; it can never, of its very nature, be quite still; it is never quite the same from one day to the next. It has its own life and its own beauty, and the creatures it nourishes are alive and beautiful also. Perhaps fishing is, for me, only an excuse to be near rivers. If so, I'm glad I thought of it."

L.H.P.: REMEMBERING A MENTOR (2021)

Leigh Perkins was CEO of the Orvis Company from his acquisition of it in 1965 until his retirement in 1992. To write about him, a man whose full life was guided by his passions for fly fishing and bird hunting until his death in May 2021, where could I possibly start? I could begin with a summary of his place on the honour roll of North American fly-fishing giants, highlighting his accomplishments, which were many and important: Articulating the outdoor community's obligation to protect the places where hunting and fishing take place and setting an example with his personal work and dedication of corporate earnings to conservation; originating the concept of fly-fishing and wing-shooting schools, thereby creating customers while also building the ranks of defenders of fish and wildlife. There are the distinctions bestowed on him by way of conservation awards and honorary degrees, and the fact that he's every outdoor person's hero for continuing to fish or hunt 250 days a year into his 90s. I could also remind you of his stature in the business world, where he is regarded as a "mail order genius" who transformed Orvis –

in 1965 a small New England company with annual sales of $500,000 – into a $90 million company under his guidance.

But those are just facts.

Instead, I'll start in my parents' front yard in Edmonton, Alberta, in the fall of 1965. I was 12. Leigh had acquired Orvis earlier that year, and shortly thereafter sent my dad a gift of a Battenkill bamboo rod, an 8-foot, 8-weight. That autumn day Leigh took me out on the lawn and taught me to double-haul with that rod. It was about the only thing he ever intentionally taught me, but it was just the first on a long list of things I learned from him.

He was in Edmonton that fall to continue a custom he'd begun several years earlier. My father was proprietor of a company that sold products made by Harris Calorific, the company for whom Leigh was sales manager in his days before Orvis. Leigh and Dad had found a common interest in bird hunting, and every year Leigh made sure his sales trip to Alberta occurred in October, which was prime time for the waterfowl and upland bird hunting they both loved. I was too young to accompany them on their hunting escapades then, but I loved to hear about them afterward, and also loved to talk to Leigh about fly fishing, with which I had recently become inexplicably fascinated. His trips to Alberta became less frequent after the acquisition of Orvis, but he kept in touch with my dad, and by association me, mostly by mail.

Leigh noticed my growing obsession with fly fishing, and even back that far encouraged it. When I was a teenager I broke the Battenkill rod on a fishing outing in Jasper National Park. I wrote Leigh a letter, apologetically telling him what had happened and asking how we could get it fixed. A few weeks later a new rod arrived in the mail to replace it.

Lynda and I were married in July 1977, and naturally – to us at least – we planned to spend our honeymoon fishing in and around Yellowstone Park. And just as naturally I wrote to Leigh, asking for suggestions on where we might fish. Along with that advice he told us to call Doug Gibson at Three Rivers Ranch, a fly-fishing lodge nearby in Idaho. We thought Doug might also suggest some good places to fish, but instead he insisted we come over to the ranch. Upon our arrival we found that they were expecting us, and we were treated like guests. After dinner at the lodge Doug took us out on the Warm River (which might have been the watershed event that securely and permanently hooked Lynda on fly fishing) and insisted we stay the night at the ranch. After packing to leave the next morning we tried to settle up but found that there was no settling up to be done. I was puzzled about this, but only for a while. I soon realized that it was all orchestrated by Leigh. I never asked him if he'd paid for it or called in a favour to our benefit, and he never said anything about it. But it was his doing. It was his way.

Much later, when my dad passed away, our family received a report from the charity we directed donations to. There, on the list of donations made in the name of Doug McLennan, was *Leigh Perkins, Manchester, Vermont.* It was his way.

When I was attending the University of Alberta in 1976, I began guiding fly fishers on the Bow River in the summers. The Bow at that time was unknown beyond Alberta. I invited Leigh to come to fish the river several times, and though he seemed sincerely interested, it didn't work out for some time. In about 1979, though, I offered again, advising that we were finding a lot of good-sized rising fish on the Bow. That did it, and in September he and son Dave arranged a single day with me.

We did a short float on the river, starting at the edge of Calgary and finishing about five miles downstream. The fishing began slowly, but I had planned to be on a particularly good dry-fly island about midday in hopes that the fish would do their thing. After lunch the daily hatch of blue-winged olives began and the fish began to rise. We spent the rest of the day there, casting to a seemingly endless supply of big rising rainbows.

When the fish started working in the quiet water behind the island, I placed myself at Leigh's shoulder, as I always did with clients. But this was different. Everything I had learned about fly fishing so far had come from books, a few friends and experience. There were no other options. But now here was a real live *expert,* casting dry flies to rising trout on my river. I watched closely as he covered rises more quickly and efficiently than I knew it could be done. Using an 8-foot, 3-inch "All Rounder," one of the original Orvis graphite rods with the spiral ridges (the "honourable scar" according to the catalog), he dropped cast after cast about two feet above the fish. I didn't know you could do that. When I cast to such fish I always made a dozen or so false casts to get everything organized and then tried to drop the fly about ten feet above the fish to avoid spooking it. But of course when I did that the fly often dragged just as it got to the fish. Leigh produced five perfect drifts over a fish in the time I would have gotten one: Deposit the fly just upstream of the fish; let it drift six feet or so; make a careful pickup and one false cast off to the side of the fish; repeat. This sequence was interrupted only when a fish took his fly, which was often. Each time this happened, Leigh set the hook and giggled with delight, but then quickly lost interest in that fish, casually dropping his rod tip to a downstream position and directing his attention back upstream to check if the other fish were still rising. He wanted to make sure there was another candidate available when he was through with this one. This, while a 20-inch rainbow was leaping and running downstream into the backing. He'd long ago come to understand that the sublime moment is the one when the fish takes the fly. It's the insatiable thirst, and a universal trait of truly experienced fly fishers.

The impacts of this day were twofold. After Leigh wrote a story about it in the *Orvis News,* the company's in-house newspaper and fly fishing's largest-circulation print publication at the time, describing it as "the best day's dry fly fishing we've ever had," word was officially out on the Bow. His story got the guiding business off the ground and fly fishers began to come. So did outdoor writers like A.J. McClane, Lefty Kreh, Charles Brooks, Ernest Schwiebert, Gary Borger and more, some at the urging of Leigh. Second, a multi-day trip to the Bow became an annual event for Leigh, who brought members of his family, friends or business associates.

Leigh would always arrive with a big pile of tackle in the rental car, and leave with a much smaller pile. Within the company he was known for generously scattering gear throughout the fly-fishing world – sometimes to the dismay of his employees. One of our guides recalled Leigh asking him at the end of the trip which rod he'd like to keep. Rick said he really liked that new Henry's Fork – an 8½-foot, 5-weight. Leigh said, "Oh-oh. That one's a prototype. I'm supposed to bring it back to the factory. I always get in trouble with the rod shop when I give away prototypes," He then added, "Ah, what the hell, they'll get over it. Here, take it and have fun with it."

One year his fishing trip to Alberta was in August. We fished the Bow and also made a side trip with a fishing pal of mine to a small stream. There he reprised his initial Alberta fly-fishing performance, catching a number of trico-eating brown trout one after another in quick succession. This happened in a much-loved piece of water that has been known since that day as the Perkins Pool. Many local fly fishers still refer to it this way; some know the story, some do not. I expect there are other Perkins Pools, Perkins Runs and Perkins Flats throughout the fly-fishing world, informally named in the same way.

It was during an October visit to Vermont in about 1980 to learn about rod building that Leigh's influence on my bird hunting took root. One afternoon we took a walk in the woods with one of his Brittanys for a brief grouse and woodcock hunt. I had hunted plenty previously, but mostly without dogs, and this day I was along as a gunless observer. The dog went on point and Leigh said, "She's got a bird pinned there. Here, take my gun and flush the bird, and you'll be able to say you shot a woodcock." I took the gun, flushed the bird and was thereafter able to say that I had shot *at* a woodcock. The shot was a miss, but the seed that was sown that day scored a direct hit. It was pointing dogs for me from then on. Leigh was one of the people I looked to for advice on canine matters. My education on this subject included Leigh's strong recommendation that a bird dog (or three or four) should live in the house with the family.

Over the years he invited me to join him on a number of outdoor adventures of one kind or another – bird hunting in Montana, fly fishing in Wyoming, quail and duck shooting in Florida. I quickly learned that the only sensible reply to these invitations was, "That sounds great. Tell me where and when and I'll be there," for I knew that whatever was on the menu should not be missed.

In about 1995 he invited me to join him to hunt grey partridge and sharp-tailed grouse for a few days with Ben Williams in Montana. After a day of great dog work and great company, we were having a drink in Ben's living room, going over the events of the day. I babbled on about what a thrill it was to hunt with two of my outdoor heroes. Then the discussion turned to the usual topics, which for Leigh and Ben meant mainly the work of the dogs. Leigh knew as much as anyone about the technical side of bird hunting – guns, loads, shooting methods – but at the end of a day he wanted to talk about birds and dogs rather than hits and misses.

It was after one of these days that my dog – a Brittany – got a little rambunctious and broke a nice vase in Ben's house. Ben and his wife Bobbie were very gracious about it, but after we left Leigh sent a bouquet of flowers to Bobbie, thanking her for her hospitality and signing the card from both of us. When I found out and thanked him for smoothing things over on my behalf, he said, "No problem. I figured you needed all the help you could get."

His time outdoors was shaped by three things. First, his immense curiosity. After a day on another Montana hunting trip he said what he always said after a day outdoors: "What a great day!" and then added, "But the best part was watching that falcon stoop on the birds we flushed. You almost never get to see that!"

Second, his relentless enthusiasm. In Florida I was among several guests joining him to hunt at his Mays Pond Plantation. After everyone had arrived he gave us a rundown of the next day's events. "We'll hunt ducks at daybreak, then come back here for breakfast. Then we'll take the quail wagon out. After lunch in the field we'll hunt quail some more, and then I've got a dove shoot lined up for late afternoon." He was 76 at the time.

Third, his sense of humour, especially when the brunt of the laughter came at his expense, as when relating to others his somewhat questionable attempt to clean ducks in my mother's kitchen sink. When that option ceased to be – uh – available, he adapted nicely and tried plucking ducks in a rental car as it raced down the highway toward the airport and his flight home – about which he later reported, "It didn't work that well. I tried to push the feathers out the window but they just got sucked back into the air vents and swirled around inside the car." For Leigh the story after the event was as important as the event itself, especially if it involved some chaos. When remembering and describing oddball things like the antics of the pet goat that lived in his house, Leigh would laugh till he almost couldn't talk. And neither could the rest of us.

Along the way he passed on his thoughts on how to engage our children in hunting and fishing. He believed that if we introduce them to these things when they're young, they'll learn to enjoy them early. They may leave them for a while when careers, spouses and perhaps their own children enter the picture, but they'll often come back to them later. Lynda and I have followed this advice with our daughter, and as we babysit her Brittany puppy tonight, I can vouch for its soundness.

Leigh Perkins is by far the largest influence on just about every part of my outdoor life, from the type of fly fishing I like best (casting dry flies to rising fish), to the type of hunting I like best (hunting prairie birds with pointing dogs), to the breeds of dogs I've owned (pointers, setters, Brittanys), to the way I cook ducks (medium rare, saving the carcasses for soup). He showed me that the essence of the outdoor experience can be found in both the expected and unexpected places. Perhaps most importantly he showed me how to enjoy hunting and fishing fully, whether the results are stellar or not. He once said, and I paraphrase, "If you're not happy with the hunting or fishing unless it turns out perfectly, you won't be happy very often. The key is to expect and appreciate partial success, because that's what we most often get."

His legacy in fly fishing, bird hunting, business and conservation is massive, widespread, enduring. Yet, when asked once what he'd most like to be remembered for, he said, "My duck soup recipe." He once also mused that if he hadn't ended up with Orvis he might have made a pretty good dog trainer.

I recently read a story in *Fly Fisherman* magazine called "Our Mount Rushmore." The article made me realize that everyone has a Mount Rushmore – a small group of people who stand above the rest in their influence and our admiration. First and tallest on my Mount Rushmore is Leigh Perkins.

Dry fly season is just starting on the Bow as I write this. I know a good spot. I'll go there and if I find some fish rising nicely I'll do my best to catch one for Leigh. I'll try to drop my fly about two feet above the rise, and if I hook up but lose the fish on the first jump, I'll laugh a little and think, *What a great day.*

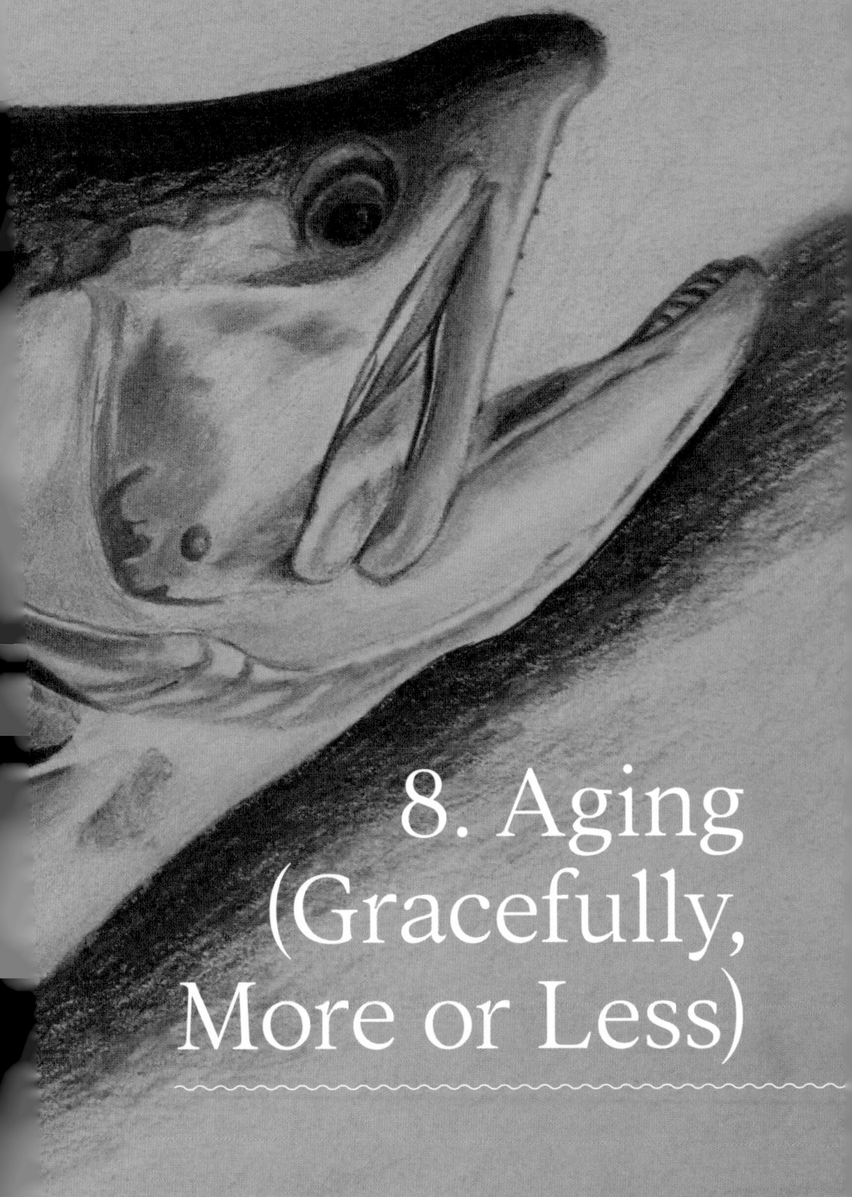

8. Aging (Gracefully, More or Less)

LONGER LUNCHES (2010)

I used to love to fish until dark. Even if I started early in the morning, it was easy to stay on the water until well after the sun was gone. It made no sense not to stay late, for the anticipation of "happy hour" – the golden period when the sun retreats behind the hills – is what kept me out there. But when the 2009 fishing season was over I noticed with some surprise that I hadn't fished until dark once. I could probably come up with several good explanations for this – that the fishing hasn't been as good at dark lately, that I'm more skilled now and don't need the advantage of evening, or that I just happened to have a lot of other commitments this summer. I might also say that while increasing age *could* have the same effect on a person, it certainly wasn't true in my case. Right. I could say any of these things, but I'd be either lying or deluding myself.

Aging is a funny thing. You don't notice it while it's happening but you sure notice it after it's happened, and the only conclusion I can draw is that it must sneak up on you when you aren't paying attention. And it may be that there are a number of predictable stages to the process, as experts tell us there are with the process of grieving.

The evidence is often revealed initially by changes in certain bodily functions, some of which we'll discuss here and some of which we won't. It often starts with the eyes. At first there's nothing more than a general sense that it may be taking a little longer than it used to to find the eye of the hook with the end of the tippet. When you first notice this there will be denial. If your older fishing partner sees you fumbling and stabbing and offers to loan you his reading glasses, you'll decline flatly, mumbling that the light is bad. He'll smile, and say something like, "Okay, have it your way, but let me know when you're ready to borrow them." It's even worse when your younger fishing companion sees you fumbling, because he may offer to change your fly for you. You'll decline this too, perhaps with a bit of an edge in your voice.

But don't worry; it'll only get worse. You'll eventually cave and start using some sort of aid to fly changing – reading glasses, sunglasses with magnifying bifocals, or the fly-threading gizmos the young guy at the fly shop offered you a little too eagerly. When I was a 20-something fly-fishing guide I often wondered why my older clients were reluctant to change flies even when it was apparent that the fish had seen the first one and weren't going to eat it. But now I'm one of those guys, and I understand. When you're over 50, changing flies is a substantial undertaking if the fly is small and/or the light is bad (or if they're not).

About the same time you'll get another annoying message from your eyes. On a late trip home from fishing one night you'll say something like this to your companion or yourself. "If we can communicate with the whole world on the Internet, why for the love of God can't somebody figure out a way to make the lines on the highway show up in the dark when it's raining?"

A couple of other body parts are likely to get your attention too, the most likely being your back, your hip, your knees or all the above. If you've pursued some type of athletic activity in your youth, you'll probably find that one or more of these components has exceeded its warranty period and doesn't work like it used to. This is the stage I'm in now. I realized it last summer when I joined some friends on a fishing trip organized to celebrate a couple of the guys' 60th birthdays. In our youth the after-fishing conversation on such a trip would have centred on fish or flies, or possibly the merits of particular trucks, cigars, sports teams or women. This time, though, I noticed that the talk was mostly a comparison of medical procedures and anti-inflammatories, and that some of us were taking notes.

And there were other things on this trip that further confirmed change. There was a great meal after fishing one day – we had some nice steaks and a bottle of wine to wash them down – and we partook of it all at the cabin while the sun was still up. The thought struck me that 25 years ago this meal would have been a bag of chips and a Coke, and it would have been consumed long after dark in a soggy tent or the cab of a pickup. This realization produced no melancholic yearnings for yesteryear.

Through my 20s and 30s I simply had to fish as much as physically possible. This included finding open water to fish in the winter. I spent many pleasant hours on the ice-free portions of the Bow and Crowsnest rivers during this time, and it added to my enjoyment and understanding of the rivers. But these days, I don't do it. And that's not because I think about going fishing and decide not to; it's because it never occurs to me to consider it. And maybe the most revealing part of this is the fact that I'm okay with it. I've apparently become more comfortable with the idea of an off-season.

When I was younger I also took pride in always being the first guy wadered up, the first guy with his fly tied on and the first guy to make a cast. Then I noticed one day that I had been transformed into the annoying guy who always gets halfway to the stream before realizing he left something back in the truck (probably his reading glasses). So, if you're a "young buck" I know you wonder a little about older guys like us, who putter around and take a long time to get organized, who want to use big flies all the time, and who want to spend more time at lunch and maybe take a nap on the bank afterward. You might even feel a little sorry for us, assuming that we've lost our edge and maybe even lost sight of the objective of the sport. And, if the objective is to make as many casts as possible and therefore to catch as many fish as possible, you might be right. But if the objective is to enjoy all aspects of a day's fishing, well, don't look now but the old guys might be ahead of you. That's because they've been through the stages, from realization, to acceptance, and finally to embracing a slower pace to fishing and life outdoors in general.

As this stage arrives the peripheral components of hunting and fishing – the setting, the companions, the food, the memories that are stirred by the activity of fishing – become every bit as important as the success of the activity itself. We can't go as long or as hard as we used to, but we also notice that this isn't so bad. The surprise is in the revelation that in an odd way, "less is more," or at least "less is just as good."

The relentless passage of time is life's Great Deception. Through the first third of your life you carry a subconscious assumption that time is an unlimited commodity. But even while time is giving you this sense, it is also undeniably proving the opposite, and you don't know you're being deceived until the deception is complete. You can't see the hour hand of a clock move, but move it does, ceaselessly, dispassionately. Those of my generation will remember the Joni Mitchell song, "The Circle Game": "We're captive on the carousel of time. We can't return, we can only look behind from where we came, and go 'round and 'round and 'round in the circle game... Take your time, it won't be long now till you drag your feet to slow the circles down."

I believe the key to aging gracefully in the outdoors is to cultivate an appreciation for the ancillary components of hunting and fishing before the time of slowing down occurs. So the lesson might be this: Even if you're young enough to go long and hard, learn to enjoy the "other things" while you're out there. Notice wild things other than fish and bugs. Figure out which small town has the best coffee shop. Carry binoculars and folding chairs in your fishing vehicle. You know, don't you, that the day is coming when these "other things" will be the main attraction to a fishing trip? And at the end of that day it will be more important to have gone fishing than to have caught fish.

OLD SCHOOL (2017)

It's hard not to notice that our sport is growing and progressing. This is as it should be. Today we know more about nearly every aspect of fly fishing than ever before: more about the fish, the things fish eat, the mechanics and physics of casting. And our gear has been on a steady upward track for the last hundred years or so.

This is good, for progress is nearly always beneficial. But something else that's also good is the fact that many things – flies, tackle, methods – that are not new (read: old-fashioned or out-of-date) are also still viable.

Take fly patterns, for example. Because we know so much more about the things fish eat and the way those things live and behave, and because we have so many innovative fly-tying materials in the hands of perhaps the most creative group of fly tiers ever, we have better imitations available to us than ever before.

But for trout at least, traditional patterns like the Adams, Gold-Ribbed Hare's Ear, Light Cahill and others still work. So do nymphs without beads (yes, they are legal) and Woolly Buggers without beads, cones, eyes, rattles, rubber legs or holographic flashabou. For you lake guys, how about two old standards from British Columbia, the Carey Special and Doc Spratley? What do they imitate? I don't know, but they caught fish before the word *chironomid* became part of the fly-fishing vernacular, and they still do.

The Adams and Gold Ribbed Hare's Ear are not especially accurate imitations of specific stages of specific insects, even if they were the best that tiers could come up with at the time. But what the old patterns have that the newer, more sophisticated patterns don't is an ability to look a little bit like a lot of things, and this makes them work in a lot of circumstances. So, as I often tell people, an Adams is never a bad choice.

"But," you might say, "these older patterns won't work on educated fish that have seen all the patterns from the local fly shops." Maybe not. But counteracting that is the fact that fly fishers get so deeply into the world of perfect imitation that they never think of throwing an Adams at an educated, selectively feeding trout on a heavily fished stream. And because most of the other anglers on that stream today and yesterday and the day before likely used the same approach, it's quite possible those trout have never seen a plain old Adams. One of the best advantages you can have in these kinds of streams is throwing something the fish have not seen. So... will it work? I don't know, but it's certainly worth a try. The best thing about using old-fashioned, out-of-date flies is the fact that nobody's told the fish they're not supposed to eat them.

The best example of a fly that is out of fashion but still effective is the oldest type of fly: the English wet fly. Soft hackle patterns and "winged wets" have been with us through the entire history of fly fishing, yet are rarely used today and are scarce in most fly-shop bins.

If they still work, why did these older flies fall out of use? My guess is that because it's simply in our nature to assume that newer is better.

And the same is true of fly-fishing methods. The down-and-across swing that is fly fishing's original method – the one used with the aforementioned wet flies – still works. Our recently acquired knowledge has shown us why. We now know that this type of presentation does a fine job of imitating the rising-to-the-surface movements of a number of emerging aquatic insects.

Then there's nymphing. I think there's been both progression and regression in this method. In the 1970s Charles Brooks wrote a book called *Nymph Fishing for Larger Trout.* In it he described multiple nymphing methods, none of which employed a strike indicator. What??? Isn't that impossible? It wasn't then and it isn't now.

Short-line nymphing, sight-nymphing and Euro-nymphing are three types of fishing that can be done effectively without indicators. Indicators are a great help for certain kinds of fishing, and for getting started in nymphing. But I encounter many fly fishers who think indicator nymphing is the only kind of nymphing. Because of this pervasive belief, indicator nymphing sometimes stalls a fly fisher's development, and that's not what most of us want.

Streamer fishing hasn't fallen out of use as much as some of the other methods, but I don't think it's as popular as it used to be. But it still works, even in places where the staple methods are nymphing and dry-fly fishing. I've spent many tough days on difficult spring creeks using 6x tippets and size 20-something dry flies to try and fool PhD trout. For a change of pace I like to put on a smallish, plain Wooly Bugger, and I'm usually able to catch a few of the fish that were nearly impossible earlier. In these places, to paraphrase Yogi Berra, I think the streamers work because nobody uses them.

I could go on, but I won't, except to say that I'm fully aware of the possibility that these words are the simple blatherings of an old guy who's in love with the past and spends too much time looking in the rear-view mirror. But, maybe not.

FISHING VICARIOUSLY (2016)

I like catching fish. I like catching them a lot (and I like catching a lot of them). But there are times when it's almost as good to watch somebody else do the catching. It's a little hard to say why this is so, but there seem to be several possibilities.

If you're helping someone learn to fly fish or learn a different way of fishing, there's satisfaction that comes with being part of their success. This is how professional guides get their fulfillment, and I think having the ability to get it from others is what makes exceptional guides exceptional. And the ones who don't have it, the ones who run out of patience, gnash their teeth and start chewing on streamside grass, don't stay in the business long.

In the previous century, when I was a guide, I was sort of a hybrid of the two. Though there were days and times when I had to bite my tongue to keep from saying, "Give me the damn rod, get out of the way and watch," I slowly learned to take satisfaction and (hopefully) quiet pride in facilitating someone else's success, realizing fairly early on that it's a more difficult undertaking and frankly a greater accomplishment to have somebody else catch a fish than to catch one yourself. And when it's done right the fisherman might come away believing he did it all himself. It's part of the guiding job to validate this, encouraging and congratulating the angler, even while knowing that you made a crucial, if unacknowledged, contribution to the success. There were times, if I was on my stroke, when I believed I could talk someone into catching a fish in spite of all the things that were conspiring to prevent it.

On one occasion I was guiding an older gentleman. We had a big group of trout rising right in front of us, but because of aging eyes, bad light and riffled water he couldn't see the fly or the rises. I was able to see them because I was in my 30s. On several occasions a fish took his fly, but because he couldn't see it he didn't set the hook and didn't get the fish. I watched for a while, wondering how to help, and eventually said, "Hand me the rod for a minute. I want to check your leader and put more floatant on the fly." When I had done that I made a lazy cast into the water. I made it look like I was just getting the line out so he could make his next cast easily, but I intentionally directed the fly right into the pod of rising fish. Sure enough, a nice trout took. My fisherman didn't see it and I said nothing, but I made a short, sharp hook-setting motion with the rod tip that also went unnoticed. I immediately handed him the rod and said, "Here you go, everything looks fine." He took the rod, raised the tip to start a backcast and felt the fish on. "Hey, I got one!" he said. In the excitement that ensued he didn't recall that I had made the cast and hooked the fish. And I didn't tell him.

These days, with guiding well behind me, I spend time teaching folks the skills of fly fishing, and the biggest kick I get is in seeing the "lightbulb" come on. Most often this is a revelation relative to casting, but sometimes it's something else, perhaps just a dialing-up of the passion-metre. Several decades ago this happened to my wife, Lynda. We were on a river a couple of hours from home and it was starting to get dark. Fish were rising, and I stopped fishing and watched her go. She caught several good fish but there were more still rising. I thought we should probably stop and begin the long, dark drive home, but she didn't want to stop. "Just a couple more casts," she said, as a prelude to approximately a hundred more casts. She had never caught this many fish in one session before, and I think it was later – quite a bit later – that we both realized the role-reversal that had just occurred.

Other times there's no teaching or coaching involved. It's simply a matter of watching somebody with great skill do their thing. My friend Jim Gilson, from Pennsylvania, is one such angler. When he puts on a pair of nymphs and steps into a good-looking run, it's worth taking a seat and ordering popcorn. The same is true of George Anderson, of Livingston, Montana. When he fishes the spring creeks near his home, it's always a show worth watching. He seems to catch fish at will, and when I ask his fishing friends how it is that he does it so easily, they shrug and say, "That's just George."

Closer to home, long-time fishing partners Rick and Thelma Harding are dry-fly specialists and when Lynda and I fish with them we often take turns on rising fish or good-looking water. One or two people fish and the others sit on the bank, watching and gently heckling or cheering for the fish. It matters little whether you're fishing or watching; the pleasure is equal.

And I guess that's the point.

MATURITY OR... (2018)

The old and the young view one another in interesting ways. When it comes to the outdoors, veteran anglers and hunters sometimes see young rookies as puzzling blurs of energy and ignorance, not exactly sure where they're going but making great time getting there. The younger crowd may consider the older guys to be past their prime, too slow, or lacking the commitment required to catch a fish or take an animal.

Clearly, how you view aging in the outdoors depends on where you lie on life's unremitting continuum – where you find yourself relative to that metaphorical piece of geography we refer to simply as "the hill" (as in "over" it).

I've now reached the point where I reluctantly admit that I've had my last look at the inclining side of the hill and now have a clear view of its opposite slope. Apparently I'm not part of the younger crowd anymore. This revelation has brought with it a slightly different perspective, and I've observed a few changes in myself. For one, I no longer have to fish or hunt when conditions are terrible. I never have and never will describe myself as a "fair weather outdoorsman," yet I realize that my outdoor ventures must carry a reasonable expectation of fun, and when it's ridiculously cold, windy, rainy or snowy, such expectation disappears. This realization has also eliminated thoughts of fishing after dark or hunting ducks in a blizzard, both projects I used to find acceptable and even appealing but which now never even occur to me.

I've also noticed that I don't need to spend as many hours hunting or fishing as I used to in order to derive a full serving of enjoyment. I was once as hard core and hard driven as anybody, gladly making a long drive to fish all day and into the night, then making the same long drive home and going to work the next morning. The objective, of course, was to maximize the "catching" part of the fishing. If a few more hours on the water produced a few more fish, that made the experience better. In those days a full day of fishing meant 12 or 14 hours on the water with a ten-minute break for lunch. Today it's about five hours on the water with an hour for lunch, plus a nap.

I also choose to fish in places where I have the best chance of fishing the way I enjoy it most, which is casting dry flies to rising trout. I've adopted the philosophy of an older fly-fishing friend who achieved this stage of enlightenment before I did, and whose mantra was, "If they're not going to eat dry flies, they can do without."

It's also true with hunting. My favourite way to spend a bright October day is to follow my pointing dogs across the prairie in search of Hungarian partridge or sharp-tailed grouse.

In recent years my attention has been drawn more to the landscape of the hunt – the way the land, sky and water looks, sounds and smells – than to the potential of heavy weight in the game-pocket of my vest. I'm as likely to choose a hunting spot based on fond recollections of previous hunts as on the current probability of finding birds. And it's easy and acceptable these days to stop a few birds short of a limit or a few hours short of sundown. It feels just as good to sit on a pretty hillside and admire the view for a few minutes as it does to shoot another bird. When it feels this good, one more bird can't make it better.

Today, in both my hunting and fishing, it seems I'm concerned increasingly more with the "how" and increasingly less with the "how many." What's surprising is that I'm finding I enjoy my time outdoors at least as much from this vantage point as I did from the other side of the hill, when I too was one of those puzzling blurs of energy and ignorance.

OLD FRIENDS (2012)

"Can you imagine us years from today, sharing a park bench quietly?
How terribly strange to be seventy."
—Paul Simon

Since fly fishing is a somewhat social pastime, most of us have companions to share it with. Maybe you have to have been at it awhile to notice this, but one of the traditions of the sport, albeit one that is being usurped by social media, the Internet and its digital cohorts, is that of the older teacher or mentor who helps a younger person along. And while this begins as a relationship between a teacher and a student, it morphs into something a little different when the student's skill catches up with the teacher's. From then on it's simply two fishing companions with a considerable difference in age. If you're 25 or 30 or 35 and you frequently fish with someone who's 15 or 20 years older than you, the age difference means almost nothing. You enjoy each other's company and you're both comfortable and capable of the physical demands that come with the sport.

But when you get a little further down the path the differ ence begins to make a difference. I've been thinking about this a lot lately, probably because I have a number of fishing and hunting companions who are older than me, and in some cases it's starting to mean something.

A number of my older fishing friends have various age-related "afflictions" that are causing them to slow down a bit. I realized this a couple of times when I arrived at the water ahead of my partner, then felt guilty about it and tried to apply a sort of retroactive grace by suggesting he take the good spot I was holding for him.

All this has caught me by surprise because recently it's been more my wont to feel sorry for myself because of the way Father Time is affecting my own body and my approach to the outdoors. Now that I've come to more or less accept myself as the old guy, it seems I've forgotten how to be the young guy.

It's sad to watch your companions' physical abilities decline, but in most cases they're okay with it and it's me who is uncomfortable. I'm still sorting through how to handle this, and so far what I've come up with is the fact that these guys seem to enjoy and appreciate fishing now as much as they ever did, or maybe even more. And we still like to fish together, so even though we both know it, there's no point in bringing up the fact that things aren't exactly the way they used to be.

A particularly bittersweet memory of this concerns a friend from New York state who came to fish with another friend and me each summer for about 15 years. Stan was at least 25 years older than us and we looked forward to his visits each summer. Stan was a great friend and an experienced fly fisher. On one of his last trips west we floated the local river, as was our custom, with Gord and I taking turns at the oars while Stan fished. Stan was in his mid-70s then, and it was this day when I suddenly realized he wouldn't be coming out to fish with us forever. Though his health seemed good, any trip – even this one – could be his last one. Perhaps this thought came when I noticed that he needed some help getting in and out of the boat and that knot-tying had become a bit of a challenge. Late in the day Gord was at the oars, Stan was in the front of the boat and I was in the back. We were working a particularly good bank with streamers, firing them into the shallows and ripping them back toward the boat. When one of Stan's casts fell a couple of feet short of the current seam that was his target, without thinking I threw my fly into the spot he had missed. I stripped it twice and the fly was stopped by a big brown trout. We landed the fish and admired it – nobody more sincerely than Stan – but all through the proceedings I kept thinking, *This was supposed to have been Stan's fish. The wrong guy caught that fish. What if this is his last day on the river?*

On a fishing trip to BC quite a few years ago I helped my 12-year-old daughter cross a little creek. When we were about halfway across we stopped and I only half-jokingly said to her, "I'm helping you cross the stream today, but someday you'll have to help me cross it." She gave me a startled look. That day's not here yet (at least according to me it's not), but as my knees creak and my back aches I can see it peering at me from the horizon.

OTHER TITLES BY JIM MCLENNAN

Blue Ribbon Bow

Trout Streams of Alberta

Fly Fishing Western Trout Streams

Water Marks: Thirty Years of Fly-Fishing Insight

Jim McLennan was one of the first fly-fishing guides on Alberta's Bow River, and is a well-known outdoor writer and speaker. *Trout Tracks* is his fifth book on fly fishing. His writing also appears frequently in outdoor publications including *Fly Fisherman* and *Fly Fusion* (for whom he is contributing editor), *Alberta Fishing Guide*, *Pointing Dog Journal*, *Strung*, *Gray's Sporting Journal*, *Anchored Outdoors* and others. Jim is co-host, along with Derek Bird, of *Fly Fusion Television*.

Lynda McLennan was a founding director of Casting For Life, a fly-fishing retreat for breast cancer survivors, and has been teaching fly fishing in various formats since the 1980s. She is a skilled photographer whose work appears in magazines, books and on numerous websites. In recent years she has taken up painting and drawing and her work illustrates *Trout Tracks*.

Jim and Lynda began fly fishing together in the 1970s. Married since 1977, they have operated McLennan Fly Fishing full time since 2004, and have taught thousands of people the fine art of fly fishing. For more information or to purchase prints of the artwork featured in *Trout Tracks*, please visit mclennanflyfishing.com